Robin Bruce Lockhart is a former newspaper executive who was Foreign Manager of the *Financial Times* before joining Beaverbrook Newspapers. Some years ago he returned to the City where he is a successful stockbroker.

Son of the late Sir Robert Bruce Lockhart, the author and former Deputy Under-Secretary of State for Foreign Affairs, he was educated in various parts of Europe before going to Cambridge University. He served in the R.N.V.R. throughout the war and before going out to the Far East as Flag Lieutenant to the British Naval Commander-in-Chief, he was doing Naval Intelligence work in France and at the Admiralty.

Robin Bruce Lockhart also paints and has exhibited in several West End galleries. His present home is in Sussex.

Robin Bruce Lockhart

Reilly – Ace of Spies

Futura
Macdonald & Co
London & Sydney

A Futura Book

First published in Great Britain in 1967
by Hodder & Stoughton Ltd

This edition published in 1983
by Futura Publications, a Division of
Macdonald & Co (Publishers) Ltd
London & Sydney
First reprint 1983

ISBN 0 7088 2003 4

Printed and bound in Great Britain by
Collins, Glasgow

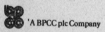 'A BPCC plc Company

Futura Publications
A division of
Macdonald & Co (Publishers Ltd)
Maxwell House
74 Worship Street
London EC2A 2EN

This book is dedicated to those
nameless and faceless heroes of
Britain's Secret Intelligence Service
whose epitaph can never be written

AUTHOR'S PREFACE TO THIS EDITION

When I learnt that filming of a TV series of the life of Sidney Reilly, based on my book, was to go ahead, I knew that one of the most difficult tasks facing the film-makers would be the selection of an actor to play Reilly – surely the most chameleon-like and many-faceted agent in the history of espionage. Although the choice of actor was not in any way my problem, I racked my brain for weeks on end trying, unsuccessfully, to think of someone who would be a success as Reilly on the screen. Shortly afterwards, Chris Burt – who had not long finished filming 'The French Lieutenant's Woman' – was appointed producer of the series and, voicing my fears that the actor who could play Reilly simply did not exist, I remarked to him over lunch one day that the ideal person for the part would have been James Mason in his youth. In the event, the role went to the award-winning Sam Neill who bears some resemblance to James Mason, has a not dissimilar voice and is a personal friend of his; moreover, Mason is one of his greatest fans. Oh happy coincidence!

Of his role, Sam Neill told me: 'Playing Reilly in the end has meant taking an imaginative leap.' I feel sure that television viewers will agree with me that Sam Neill is a great jumper. And his passionate feeling for the down-trodden Poles, aroused after filming in Poland, has a great deal of that fierce intenseness which was one of the most dominant of Sidney Reilly's characteristics.

As a teenager, I had the peculiar experience of watching Leslie Howard portray my father, while he was alive, in the Warner Brothers film 'British Agent'. It was with equally eerie emotions that I saw my father come to life again in the form of Ian Charleson – one of the stars of 'Chariots of Fire' – bestriding the set as Reilly's colleague at E.M.I.'s Elstree Studios. Ian tells me that as a Scot himself he was well able to understand the conflicting Highland and Lowland traits in my father's character.

Not a few authors, despite satisfied egos when their books are turned into films or TV series, cavil that their brainchildren have been emasculated by film producers into pale shadows of their original work. If the TV series 'Reilly – Ace of Spies' has added to and subtracted a certain amount from my account of the master spy's career in order to heighten the dramatic effect on the screen, I have been delighted that the scripts adhere to the basic content of my book. Having lived and breathed Sidney Reilly while researching and writing the book, it has been an exhilarating adventure for me to watch the TV series take shape.

On first publication, the book aroused considerable excitement in the press throughout the world – not least in Russia where Isvestia considered it as additional evidence of Reilly's work against the Soviets. The reviewers were generally adulatory in their comments and the book has been translated into a number of languages and even serialised in a Greek newspaper. 'Out-bonds Bond' and 'Out-philbies Philby' were comments made by several critics. 'Makes Cicero, Mata Hari and James Bond look veritable novices', 'Makes James Bond look a piece of nonsense', 'Stranger than 007 fiction' were other remarks. Several expressed the view that the story of Reilly would make an exciting movie hit. In Russia there have been at least one stage play, one film and one TV series devoted to Sidney Reilly and 'The Trust' and to what the Russians call 'The Lockhart Plot'. Now television viewers the world over can see a British version.

The last years of Reilly's life are still veiled in mystery and for about two years after my book came out I received literally hundreds of letters from all over the world from readers who claimed to have met or seen Reilly in various disguises or who came up with new theories about his later life. The TV series ends with one of several different 'solutions' put out by the Russians and to which I refer in my book. However, I am far from satisfied that it is the truth. Over the past ten years or more I have made a number of further efforts to try to determine once and for all the ultimate secret of Reilly's life but to no avail. It can only be known in Russia – if it is known at all – but, as one Russian who could well have been in a position to know said to me: 'The records have probably been destroyed' and, I suspect, very possibly the men who had access to the Reilly files may themselves have been destroyed by Stalin. To quote from the last paragraph of my book: '(Reilly's fate) is probably destined to be for ever shrouded in mist.'

Although I am no film technician, having watched Chris Burt and his two directors, Jim Goddard and Martin Campbell, at work backed up by a second-to-none production team, I came to appreciate the sheer craftsmanship involved in bringing Reilly into your homes. I think that all engaged in the making of the series agree that it has been the most exciting production on which they have ever worked.

If you are enjoying or have enjoyed the television series, you will surely enjoy the book which tells the full story of Sidney Reilly so far as it is known. If you are fascinated by Reilly after reading the book, you will surely be fascinated by the TV series.

Hove   Robin Bruce Lockhart
Sussex.   1983

PREFACE

'The greatest spy in history' . . . 'One of the most amazing men of his generation' . . . 'One of the bravest men of his time' . . . 'Almost incredible' . . . 'No more amazing story has ever before been revealed'. These are but a few of the comments newspapers have applied to Sidney Reilly, the master spy – the man who was said to possess eleven passports and a wife to go with each.

To the intelligence services of the world, including the chiefs of the British Secret Service, who were his employers, Sidney Reilly was a man of mystery, a man who lived for danger, who spoke seven languages and who arrived on the international espionage scene from an unknown background. No-one, not even his employers, was certain either of his true nationality or his real name. To all who knew him he was a man of many parts but essentially an enigma, who apparently disappeared from the world as mysteriously as he had entered it. His closest friends described him as 'sinister'; his enemies were forced to acknowledge both his exceptional daring and his compelling charm. He gambled with death with the same regularity as he visited casinos and gaming clubs. Few women could resist him.

Although the press announced Sidney Reilly's death at the hands of the Russian Secret Police in September,

7

1925, reports that he was still alive were subsequently received from many places. These reports persisted until 1945, after which – silence.

For years the truth about the master spy has been a mystery not only to the general public but also to the secret services of many countries.

Newspapers throughout the world have published fantastic stories of Reilly's dramatic spying activities. Before the last war, French newspaper readers were entertained by an enthralling strip cartoon of his exploits. Most of these newspaper tales owed more to the imagination of the writers than to anything else. Through the years both the British and Russian Governments, perhaps understandably, have remained largely silent about Reilly's career.

In 1931, Pepita Reilly, Sidney Reilly's third wife, published a highly melodramatic book with the title *The Adventures of Sidney Reilly, Britain's Master Spy.* Covering a short period of Reilly's life, it purported to be a narrative begun by Reilly himself and completed by his wife. In fact, the book had been ghosted by a journalist and at the time of publication the *Daily Mail* commented with some truth: 'Whether it is all fact and contains no fiction may be questioned by those who knew him well.' Pepita Reilly was herself only too aware of the short-comings of the book and years later she wrote: 'I would like to write a new version without all the melodrama "my" book has been turned into.' And yet my father, Sir Robert Bruce Lockhart, K.C.M.G., whose name was bracketed with Reilly's in the famous 'Lockhart Plot' to assassinate Lenin and who knew Reilly intimately for a number of years, in commenting on Pepita's book, wrote: 'There are episodes in Reilly's life which are even more astonishing than those recounted in this book.'

I, myself, knew Sidney Reilly only when I was a small boy in Prague, but throughout my life he has been an object both of mystery and of fascination. Much of my youth was spent in Europe and to a great extent the drama of the Russian Revolution, with which my father's career had been intimately concerned, dominated my youthful imagination. Whenever my parents received visitors – statesmen, ex-statesmen, would-be statesmen, diplomats and others whose activities on the international scene were rather more mysterious, Russia was invariably a major topic of conversation. Nearly always the shadowy figure of master spy Sidney Reilly would crop up in any discussion on Bolshevism. Many of our family friends had been or were still concerned with intelligence work of one kind or another and sometimes, after a guest had departed, my parents would spellbind me with an absorbing tale of some exciting spying mission the guest had undertaken. However, none of these visitors, I would be assured, could compare as a spy with Sidney Reilly.

As a boy I used to listen entranced to Sir Paul Dukes recounting some of his extraordinary adventures as a spy. His sensitive face and his long tapering musician's hands seemed strangely inconsistent in a man who, as a top agent of Britain's Secret Service, travelled the steppes of Russia disguised as a Red soldier or a railway worker. But although Dukes was a boyhood hero of mine, neither he nor the other spies I met ever measured up to the stature of Sidney Reilly. I could never find out enough about Reilly – what anyone knew was little enough – and I was resolved that one day I would unravel the mystery of the master spy.

When the Second World War broke out, I soon found myself mixed up in intelligence matters and it was while working for the Naval Intelligence Division at the Admiralty that I first met Ian Fleming, the creator of James Bond. Fleming was personal assistant to Rear Admiral J. H. Godfrey, C.B., the Director of Naval Intelligence, but when France was collapsing before the German *blitzkrieg* it was I who was detailed to 'rescue' Admiral Godfrey's daughter, who was caught in France, and bring her safely to England. It was a journey not without its excitement but, at the time, I could not help reflecting that a man such as Sidney Reilly would have come home not only with the admiral's daughter but with the complete German order of battle as well!

During the war I came across many secret agents, some of whom lived dangerously and some whose missions, though important, were relatively free from danger. In particular, I was envious of one friend of mine in our Secret Intelligence Service who spent most of the war in Switzerland. But even he carried a beautifully made miniature automatic strapped to his sock suspender. Few lived as dangerously as Reilly had done.

Sidney Reilly was not only a spy. He was often as familiar with enemy spying activities as his own, although spy-catching was properly the work of M.I.5, our counter-intelligence organization. Even if its work is normally less dangerous than that of the Secret Intelligence Service, I have always had a great respect for M.I.5 since I once became briefly entangled with it as a suspect! Not long after the fall of Holland in the Second World War, an M.I.5 agent had seen me drinking in a London night-club with Prince Bernhard of the Netherlands. At the time, Prince Bernhard was suspected of pro-Nazi tendencies and for the next three weeks my every movement was watched without my knowledge!

It was while serving on the commander-in-chief's staff in the Far East before the Japanese war broke out that I first came into contact with those working on what is known as 'Y' intelligence, the interception and deciphering of enemy messages. Their work was of profound importance and I had nothing but admiration for the long-haired mathematicians and Japanese scholars who, working in offices surrounded by barbed wire, 'broke' the Japanese ciphers. Singapore was riddled with Japanese agents many of whom worked under cover as professional photographers and barbers. I used to have my hair cut by a Japanese agent and one of my war trophies is a portrait taken of me by a leading Japanese spy. It was in Singapore, too, that I married my first wife, who was secretary to the head of our Secret Intelligence Service in the Far East. Many of our secret agents in the Far East were Chinese who ran the Japanese gauntlet disguised as coolies and delivered messages on rice-paper concealed inside bamboo canes. I do not think that either the British or the Americans had an agent in Japan of even half the calibre of Sidney Reilly.

Quite recently I met the woman who had been the personal secretary to Admiral Canaris, the head of the German Secret Service. From her and her husband, the ace German spy known as 'El Koenig', I heard many amazing stories of the ingenuity of Hitler's spies. None, however, were as dramatic as the saga of Sidney Reilly's feats.

Today, the business of spying has become highly technical. In the age of the technocrat, there is little or no opportunity for the individual spy to bring off a master coup which could change the course of history. Today, much of the work of our Secret Intelligence Service is done by bowler-hatted gentlemen in Whitehall who catch the six-five p.m. every evening from Waterloo to their homes in the green belt. During the day they are busy piecing together an ever-expanding jigsaw. The pieces of the jigsaw are the scraps of intelligence which reach London from agents abroad – a network of pawns spread far around the world.

Never, in either of the two world wars – or since – have I come across or heard of any secret agent operating for any country whose exploits have come anywhere near to rivalling those of Sidney Reilly. Even in the realms of spy-fiction few more dramatic stories can have been told. When Ian Fleming wrote his first James Bond book, he was working as foreign manager of *The Sunday Times*. At the time, I was myself foreign manager of *The Financial Times* and I shall always remember Ian Fleming's comment when I telephoned to congratulate him on the sales of his book. He seemed curiously unexcited about his success and said: 'James Bond is just a piece of nonsense I dreamed up. He's not a Sidney Reilly, you know!'

Since the war many stories have been published of the men and women who worked for the resistance movements or who were dropped in enemy occupied territory to undertake sabotage operations: incredibly brave men such as Wing Commander Yeo-Thomas, G.C., M.C., better known as The White Rabbit, whom I knew in France. But the praises of the agents of our Secret Service remain inevitably unsung. Their sole recognition is the knowledge that they have done their duty.

For a long time, I have felt that if the mystery with

which Sidney Reilly's whole life has been surrounded could only be unravelled and reality separated from myth, the true story of this quite incredible man, who juggled with history itself, should be made public. He was surely not only the master spy of this century but of all time.

I make no apologies for a certain lack of completeness in this biography. The life of Sidney Reilly was too full of secrets, he had a passionate will to experience and his adventures, bringing him into touch with diverse sects of people, were too numerous. The writing of this book has been something of a major intelligence operation in itself. The story of the search for, of the finding and of the sifting and fitting together of the many different pieces in the complicated jigsaw which makes up the picture of Reilly and his life would almost make a book on its own. I have had to contend with the Official Secrets Act. The records of our Secret Intelligence Service are few and not easily prised open. I have set down only that which I know or have been able to uncover and verify as best I could. I have tried to portray something of the man himself – no easy task when writing of someone who had so many contradictory traits in his character and was different things to different people.

Reilly had no use for cynics and doubters who, he maintained, were only happy in making the world as barren for others as they had made it for themselves. He was a man who sweated both by the soul and by the body. His great pleasure in life was to do what others said was impossible. He was proof incarnate to truth being stranger than fiction.

I owe much more gratitude than I can adequately express to a great many people who have made this book possible. Without assistance from Reilly's friends and former associates this book could never have been written. My warmest thanks are due to Major Stephen Alley, M.C., Mrs. Eleanor Bishop, Baroness Budberg, Sir Robert Bruce Lockhart, K.C.M.G., The Hon. Randolph Churchill, M.B.E., Sir Paul Dukes, K.B.E., Mrs. Pepita Haddon-Chambers, Alfred F. Hill, A. F. Kerensky, Sir Reginald Leeper, G.B.E., K.C.M.G., Mrs. Loudon McLean, George Nicolson, Major-General Sir Edward Spears, Bart., K.B.E., C.B., M.C., Colonel D. S. Talbot and many others who must remain anonymous. Above all, I am grateful to Brigadier G. A. Hill, D.S.O., O.B.E., M.C., an intimate colleague of Sidney Reilly, whose help and guidance have proved invaluable throughout the preparation of this book.

Ditchling,   R. N. Bruce Lockhart
Sussex.   *July 1967*

Part One

I

With these dark words I begin my tale.

WORDSWORTH

The road was long and unlovely. The car was long and, by 1917 standards, sleek. In the half-light of the Bavarian dusk, an observer, had there been one, would have but dimly discerned that both occupants of the car wore uniform. When the car slowed down and stopped by a small, dense cluster of pine trees immediately to the right of the deserted road, he might have noted that the be-medalled passenger in the rear wore a colonel's uniform while his driver was dressed as a corporal.

The corporal turned, spoke briefly to his passenger, then opened the door and got out. He walked back to the boot, which he opened, and took out some tools. Returning to the front of the car he opened the bonnet and started tinkering with the engine. For three minutes perhaps there was quiet except for the occasional sound of metal tapping against metal. Then the driver lifted his head.

'Herr Oberst!' His voice rang out across the silent evening. 'The Herr Oberst would be most obliging if he would assist for just one small moment. There is a loose connection in the electrical circuit. If the Herr Oberst would be so very kind as to get out of the car and just hold a small nut in place while I deal with the other end of the cable, the car will be running again in no time at all.'

The colonel whose uniform looked both smart and commanding even in the twilight, got out of the car, drew off his leather gloves, which he placed carefully on the running board, and bent down to peer inside the engine. He stared at the spot to which the driver was pointing with a greasy finger.

If the colonel felt the heavy spanner which cracked his skull as he peered at the magneto, it could only have been for a fraction of a second.

The driver wiped his hands, carefully stripped the colonel of all his clothing, which he laid neatly in the boot of the car. To make quite sure the colonel was dead, he placed his thumbs on either side of the officer's windpipe and squeezed. When he was satisfied, he relaxed the pressure and, hoisting the naked body over his shoulders, he disappeared into the trees. The light was poor but the corporal was obviously familiar with his surroundings. He made his way to a small clearing in the centre of the copse and here he dropped the colonel's body. He pulled aside a large branch, thick with pine needles, which lay on the ground, to uncover a freshly dug grave. A small spade lay at the bottom of the pit.

It took less than five minutes for the corporal to strip off his own clothing, place it on the officer's corpse, roll the body into the grave and fill it in with the spade. He then re-covered the spot with the pinetree branch.

The naked driver trotted quietly back to the roadside. From the edge of the trees, he listened carefully for a minute or two, then stepped out on to the road and returned to the car. From the boot, he extracted the colonel's clothing and retired once more to the edge of the trees and proceeded to dress. The boots pinched a little but everything else seemed to fit perfectly.

From under the driver's seat, the corporal turned colonel pulled out what looked like a large tobacco pouch. With the aid of its contents and the use of the driving mirror, he made some simple but effective alterations to his facial appearance. The light was almost gone, but he had practised his disguise so thoroughly that he could have made the changes equally as well in total darkness.

At the headquarters of the German High Command the sun shone brightly as the clock struck ten. At the great rectangular table in the large conference room were assembled, together with their principal aides, the galaxy of field-marshals, generals and admirals who controlled Germany's armed forces; Von Hindenburg, Ludendorff, Von Scheer, Hipper – all were there, as well as a man with a pointed beard and a withered arm, His Imperial Majesty Kaiser Wilhelm II.

The chairs round the conference table were all occupied save one. The meeting had been in progress nearly half an hour but the representative of Prince Rupprecht of Bavaria's staff had not yet arrived. Von Hindenburg was scowling: it was inexcusable for so junior an officer not to be on time.

The clock had barely finished the last stroke of ten when the door of the conference room was thrown open. A click of heels, a smart salute and the absentee officer strode into the room. With a hangdog look on his face, the colonel apologized profusely for being late. On the journey up from Bavaria, his driver had been taken ill; he had had to drop him off in hospital and drive the rest of the way himself.

With a nod of greeting to one or two of his colleagues, the colonel sat down in the vacant chair . . . Sidney Reilly had joined the counsels of the German High Command.

II

What is your parentage?
Above my fortune, yet my state is well.

TWELFTH NIGHT

Sidney Reilly, to give him the name by which he came generally to be known, was born in South Russia, not far from Odessa, on March 24th, 1874. His mother was Russian of Polish descent; his father, apparently, a colonel in the Russian army with connections at the court of the Tsar. The family were Catholic landowners and of the minor aristocracy, but although in later years Reilly was occasionally forthcoming to one or two close friends about his origins and background, he never divulged his family name. His Christian name was Georgi. Brought up as befitted someone of his class, he and his sister Anna, two or three years older than himself, were instructed by private tutors in history, mathematics, languages and in the arts of becoming gentlefolk.

From an early age, young Georgi showed an above average ability in his studies; his curiosity on all subjects could never be assuaged. He had an uncanny aptitude for languages and in later life would frequently refer to a remark of the Holy Roman Emperor Charles V, which his tutor used to quote: 'To know another language is to possess another soul.' Deeply aware of God, he received his religious instruction from an uncle, a Catholic priest in Odessa. By the age of thirteen, he had acquired a passion for swordsmanship and, with the épée, he would best boys several years older than himself – even young army cadets. Two or three years later he took up pistol shooting to reveal a marksmanship quite remarkable in one so young.

The young spy-to-be adored both his mother and his sister and held his father in the respect due to a colonel in the army and the head of the household. He seemed destined for a military career but, as he grew older, he developed a persistent habit of arguing stubbornly with his elders and betters, which was scarcely a good trait for a potential army officer. Whatever the subject, Georgi refused to accept the opinions of his parents. His thirst for knowledge was unquenchable. Sometimes, in a discussion, he would fly into a violent temper and gesticulate with his arms as he tried to make his point. Anna would reproach him for his demonstrative ways and for behaving more like a Jew or an Italian than a young Russian gentleman.

When Georgi was fifteen, his mother fell seriously ill and his father summoned from Vienna a Jewish physician who, once before, had nursed her back from the deathbed to full health. Georgi at once struck up a great friendship with the doctor, a much travelled man whose stories of life in the various capitals of Europe aroused his interest. Georgi learnt for the first time that there were other ways of living besides the Russian way. As a youth, he found the hardest thing to believe was that people would fight to stay in a rut but not to get out of it. He developed a longing to converse with young men from other countries. The prospect of the narrow existence of a Russian army officer no longer appealed to him and, as soon as his mother's health had improved, he asked to be allowed to go to Vienna to study medicine. Despite considerable family opposition, Georgi's tenacity of purpose won the day. To Vienna he went for a three-year course in the then young science of chemistry, which his mother's doctor had recommended as a more rewarding subject than medicine.

Georgi revelled in the student life of Vienna. He enjoyed the cosmopolitan atmosphere, sensing that in both professors and fellow students he had found people with whom he was mentally and spiritually more in tune. Georgi was a model student who applied himself with diligence to his studies and eschewed the debauched life of wine and women pursued with equal diligence by so many other students. The Viennese doctor who had looked after his mother kept a benevolent eye on him and the bond of friendship which had arisen in Russia between the colonel's son and the doctor was firmly cemented as time passed. Georgi would delight in the animated discussions that took place in the doctor's house after working hours.

It was, perhaps, inevitable that Georgi should become involved in student political life. The different standards of living between the rich and poor was an anomaly in life for which he could find no satisfactory explanation. And it was not long before he joined a small university society with socialist aims called 'The League of Enlightenment'. This little band of intellectual young men used to meet weekly to discuss current affairs and to drink coffee. It seemed a very innocuous organization, until the day came when Georgi received a cable from his father. His mother was extremely ill; would he please return home at once. Georgi's spirits sank when he remembered that the doctor, who had twice before saved his mother's life, was away travelling in France and would not return to Vienna for another month.

Having packed his bags and with time to spare before his train left, Georgi went to say goodbye to some of his friends. In so doing, he ran into the secretary of the League of Enlightenment who, on hearing that Georgi was leaving for Russia, asked him to deliver a letter to Odessa. The letter was urgent and, as the Russian customs officials were so stupid, would Georgi mind sewing it in the lining of his coat? Glad of the chance to do something practical for the League, however small, Georgi readily agreed. Had his mind not been mainly filled with anxiety for his mother, he might perhaps have questioned the rather facile reason for the letter being sewn into his coat.

On his arrival in Odessa, the nineteen-year-old Georgi was promptly arrested by Ochrana* agents and thrown into gaol, accused of taking part in a revolutionary conspiracy. Despite a week's solitary confinement in a windowless cell with no sustenance except some black bread and water, he stubbornly protested his innocence. He had no idea of the contents of the letter, nor had he even met the man to whom it should have been delivered.

The League of Enlightenment, however, was not all it seemed. Its innocuous appearance cloaked an inner circle of Marxists. The letter Georgi carried did indeed relate to a revolutionary conspiracy and had it not been

* The Tsarist forerunner to the Cheka, G.P.U. and N.K.V.D. The Ochrana was a special corps of police formed 'for the investigation of all movements directed against the state and their destruction'.

for considerable string-pulling by his family Georgi would certainly have been despatched to Siberia.

When he eventually reached home, Georgi was shattered to learn that his mother had died while he had been in prison. The whole family was assembled for the funeral but, with the exception of Anna, his relations were more concerned about the disgrace Georgi had brought on the family name than about his mother's death. Anna apart, there was no consolation for the boy who had lost his mother – only recriminations. His father was strangely silent.

It was on the day of Georgi's release from prison that one of his uncles, who appeared the most disgusted of all at the young man's embroilment with the Ochrana, made the revelation which was to provide the motivating force throughout Georgi's life. It was then that the embryo Sidney Reilly began to take shape. To the assembled family, his uncle exclaimed:

'What can you expect from a dirty little Jewish bastard!'

The secret, so carefully guarded by the family for nineteen years, was out. Georgi was not his father's son at all but the offspring of an adulterous relationship between his mother and Dr. Rosenblum, the Jewish doctor who had attended her and whom Georgi had so much admired. For the sake of the family name, Georgi had been brought up as one of them, but, so said his uncle, it was obvious that bad blood would out. His name was not even Georgi but Sigmund, through a whimsical deference the family had made to a wish expressed by Dr. Rosenblum.

The whole world of Georgi suddenly collapsed. His Catholic mother whom he had loved so much had totally betrayed him. It came home to him with one sudden shocking realization that he was not even a Russian – just a miserable Jew! His father was not his father at all, his sister was not his sister. He was a mere bastard and a Jewish one at that. He remembered how often he himself had used the common Russian greeting: 'God save the Tsar and damn the Jews!'

Silently, ignoring Anna who tearfully implored him to speak to her, Sigmund Rosenblum foreswore his family. Going to his room, he took pen and paper and wrote two letters. They were brief and to the point. To Dr. Rosenblum he wrote: 'May your soul rot in the hell of loneliness'; to Anna: 'You can look for me under the ice of Odessa New Harbour.' Many years later, he said he could never forget what he had written on this occasion. In later life, the words would often haunt him in his dreams.

Leaving the house, the dazed young man went straight to Odessa where he posted his letters. In a second-hand clothes shop he exchanged his fine suit for some workman's clothes and, with the help of a sailor he met on the waterfront, he stowed away aboard a British ship in the harbour – a ship bound for South America.

At sea – the sea that led everywhere but left behind so much – the stowaway was soon discovered and hauled before the captain. With a bravado which in the circumstances seemed stubbornly obtuse, he gave his real name for the first time – Rosenblum – and announced himself to be a Jew. It was as if he derived some masochistic pleasure from the jeering and humiliation to which he was subjected.

Rosenblum spent over three years in South America, most of the time in Brazil. There he worked as a docker, on the road, on a plantation, as a cook and, for a short period, as doorman at a brothel in one of the shadier quarters of Rio de Janeiro. All the time, he was haunted by one dominant thought; that he was a Jew, a bastard and had been betrayed by his mother. And all the time, although he was not aware of it, the character of the future Sidney Reilly was being forged.

In 1895, three British army officers came to Brazil to explore the hinterland of jungle which lay up the Amazon. Rosenblum, who by now had mastered the Portuguese language and merely called himself Pedro, was engaged as cook to the expedition. An ill-fated expedition it was. Up the Amazon, hostile natives soon caused some of the bearers to desert. The native guide and the remaining bearers stayed on for a few days, but, when all three British officers went down with fever, the natives decided to kill them in their sleep and make off with stores and guns.

There are few parts of the world where nature is so intensely restless at night as in the jungles of Brazil but, amid the roars, calls and chatters in the forest, a dozing Pedro picked out the human sound of natives creeping through the scrub. Snatching up one of the officers' revolvers, he beat off the attack single-handed with his expert marksmanship. Of the British officers, one died of fever, like many explorers before and since, and was buried in the swamps of Brazil. It was Pedro who led the other two officers back through the jungle to Rio.

By the time they reached Rio, Pedro had revealed something of himself. He admitted that his real name was Rosenblum and that he had originally come to Brazil from Russia. The British, who owed their lives to someone they believed to be a Portuguese cook, were amazed at the young man who spoke several languages so fluently and was obviously well educated.

Who his family was or how he came to be in Brazil he refused to say, but in gratitude for saving his life and leading them out of the jungle, Major Fothergill, the leader of the British party and a wealthy man, gave him a cheque for £1,500. It was Fothergill, too, who somehow fixed up Rosenblum with a British passport and arranged for the young man to accompany him by ship back to England.

For the bastard of Odessa, for whom life had seemed so meaningless those past three years, life once again held possibilities.

In London, the twenty-two-year-old Rosenblum rapidly merged himself into the life of his new British friends. In the clubs of St. James's, his natural charm, which was to be one of his greatest assets through life, usually overcame the prejudice against his Jewish name. He described himself as being of German origin and shed the name Sigmund by changing its diminutive 'Siggi' into 'Sidney'.

The new Sidney Rosenblum spent freely at the tailors and shirtmakers. He became fastidious in his dress and people in the street looked twice at the elegant young man with the olive skin, blue-black hair and piercing brown eyes. He visited the Empire, dined at Frascati's and went to the gaming tables, where he played for high stakes, winning more often than he lost. He had a brief and tempestuous love affair with a prostitute called Ruby. The grudge against life which he had felt in South America seemed to be disappearing.

In the style in which Sidney – as he now called

himself – lived, even £1,500 could not last. He began to fret for his future but he rejected point-blank Major Fothergill's suggestion that he make a trip to Russia 'for the British Intelligence Service' with which Fothergill said he had 'connections'. The thought of seeing Russia again was too painful. At the same time, the realization that his money must soon run out worried him and, to forget his cares, he threw himself head-long into another love affair with a woman a few years older than himself who was just beginning to make a name for herself in London as a writer.

With Rosenblum's last £300 the couple went off to Italy. Here under the Mediterranean sun and under the influence of the Roman Catholic religion, which touched every facet of Italian life and awoke emotion-ally charged memories of his Catholic upbringing, Sidney bared his soul to his mistress. It was one of the rare occasions in his whole life when Rosenblum revealed details of his past. Finding she loved him none the less for being both half-Jewish and illegit-imate, his innate self-confidence, which had in great measure returned with his arrival in England, soared even more. He was not angry when she later published a novel,* much praised by the critics, which was largely inspired by his early life.

The young lovers visited Elba where Rosenblum's

---

* *The Gadfly* by Ethel Lilian Voynich, published by Heinemann in 1897. Although she wrote other books, the author was never to repeat the success of *The Gadfly*, her first book. Curiously enough, since the Second World War, there has been an enormous sale of *The Gadfly* behind the Iron Curtain. In Russia, the name of E. L. Voynich is bracketed with Shakespeare and Dickens as being among Britain's greatest writers. She married a Polish revolutionary who fought for Poland's freedom from Russian rule and died in New York in 1960 at the age of ninety-six.

imagination was fired by thoughts of Napoleon's achievements. In Rome, for over £100, which he could ill afford, he bought the original drawings for the Arc de Triomphe by the architect Chalgrin, with comments and criticisms written in one corner in Napoleon's own hand. Although he acquired many more valuable pieces later, this was the 'founder' piece of what was to become the well-known Reilly collection of Napoleana, a collection destined to be eventually sold to provide funds for a counter-revolution against the Bolshevik Government of Soviet Russia.

Napoleon had become Rosenblum's God and the seeds of a burning and ruthless ambition were sown. In Italy, his eager mind delved astutely into local politics; he sent Fothergill a brilliant appreciation of the Italian political situation. In Florence, he deserted his mistress, telling her he had received an important business summons from England. He returned to London.

From his lengthy report on Italy, Fothergill, who was in fact employed by the British Secret Service, and his chief realized that as well as the other assets of which they were already aware, Rosenblum possessed acute powers of political observation. Although only a very young man, they saw in him a potential agent of very high calibre.

To the surprise of both 'C' – the pseudonym in official circles for the head of Britain's Secret Service – and Fothergill, they found Rosenblum a changed man. Since his visit to Italy, he was not only willing to go to Russia but eager to do so, provided he was not asked to do anything which might be harmful to his own country.

III

Then wander o'er city and sea and land.

SHELLEY

In 1897, Rosenblum embarked on his first official assignment for the British Secret Service. At the time, it was considered a relatively unimportant mission – a try out for the new recruit. As a check on reports reaching London from the British Embassy in St. Petersburg, Rosenblum was to find out what were Russia's ambitions, if any, towards Persia, where exploratory surveys had indicated that oil might soon be discovered.

The young man, who four years previously had slunk out of Odessa desperate with shame, returned to Russia confident in his new role of British secret agent. His reports to London were to the point. Russia was developing oil at Baku in the Caucasus and was only interested in her 'fair share' in northern Persia which he recommended should be admitted. He also sent in a comprehensive report on the Trans-Siberian Railway which had been completed as far as Lake Baikal.

In Russia, too, the latest recruit to Britain's Secret Intelligence Service found a new mistress. A twenty-three-year-old red-headed beauty, she was Margaret

31

Thomas, a tourist from England accompanied by her recently acquired sixty-year-old husband – a non-conformist minister from Wales. Margaret looked bored but desirable and Hugh Thomas, her husband, appeared surprisingly wealthy for a minister. The great difference in their ages spoke for itself. Admittedly the presence of the husband was a bit awkward, but Rosenblum was not to be deterred by such a trifling inconvenience. He accompanied the Thomases as they crossed Europe by easy stages on their return to England. The minister slept very soundly and, in the various hotels at which they stayed, suspected nothing though Rosenblum's bedroom always lay directly across the corridor from the one he shared with his wife.

Back in London, Hugh Thomas and Margaret returned to their house at 6, Upper Westbourne Terrace, Paddington – Rosenblum to rooms at 3, Cursitor Street, Holborn. 'C', who had been well satisfied with his new agent's reports, had another mission lined up for him, but Rosenblum astounded him by turning down all further assignments for the time being. He said he had important matters to which he had to attend, the nature of which he refused to reveal. He intended taking indefinite leave. He would report for duty again when he had completed his private business.

Rosenblum's 'business' was Margaret. He became a regular visitor to Upper Westbourne Terrace and the visits were more frequent when Hugh Thomas fell ill. Rosenblum, the doctor's son, the chemistry student, came to the fore. His knowledge of medicine seemed greater than that of the doctor; he brought his own special prescriptions from the chemist. The health of the minister did not improve.

On March 4th, 1898, Hugh Thomas made a will at

Upper Westbourne Terrace leaving all his estate to Margaret. A few days later, despite Hugh Thomas's serious condition, the strange decision was taken that the Thomases and Rosenblum should all go to Europe. They spent a couple of days packing but got no farther than Newhaven where, on March 13th, at the London and Paris Hotel, Hugh Thomas died. The death certificate, signed by the local doctor, gave the cause of death as: 'Morbus Cordis Syncope'.*

Margaret inherited the house at Upper Westbourne Terrace and £8,000 and on August 22nd of the same year, she and Rosenblum were married at the Holborn Register Office. The bridegroom gave his name as Sigmund Georgjevich Rosenblum and called himself a 'Consulting Chemist' but both parties to the marriage somewhat elevated the status of their parents. Rosenblum described his father as a 'Landed Proprietor' while Margaret entered her father as 'Edward Reilly Callahan, deceased, Captain in the Navy'. It was Margaret, however, who was the bigger liar of the two. Prior to her marriage to Hugh Thomas, she had been his Irish maidservant at the house in Upper Westbourne Terrace. The certificate of her marriage to Thomas described her father rather more correctly and simply as 'Seaman'.

After a brief honeymoon in Brussels and Ostend, the newly-weds lived in the house in Upper Westbourne Terrace, but in a style more befitting their recently acquired wealth. Neighbours spoke of 'the dark sinister gentleman who calls himself a Russian count'. They went out riding in a coach and pair. They kept a page, one Jim Browning, who wore shiny brass buttons and white gloves.

* Heart failure.

'C' had long since given up hope of employing Rosenblum again, believing him to have retired to enjoy a rich and idle life. However, as 'C' was shortly to find out, this assessment was very wide of the mark. Behind the facade of idleness and in between enjoying the new-found pleasures of married life, the restless mind of Rosenblum was busy scheming. Within a few months of his marriage, Rosenblum had persuaded Margaret to sell the house in Paddington. It was more fashionable to live near Westminster, he claimed, and on May 9th, 1899, the couple moved into rented rooms in St. Ermin's Chambers, Caxton Street, S.W. The proceeds of the sale of the house, together with Margaret's inheritance money, were placed in a new bank account in their joint names.

It was over a year since 'C' had heard from Rosenblum and he was much surprised when, in the summer of 1899, Rosenblum telephoned and asked for an urgent appointment. None the less he found time to see him the same day. On reaching 'C's' office and without waiting to exchange polite formalities, Rosenblum curtly announced that his business was complete and that he was ready to work again.

His piercing brown eyes shone even more brightly than usual from under his long black lashes. 'C', taken aback, could only presume that Rosenblum had suddenly lost all his money at gambling. He stalled, saying that he had no mission immediately available but that he would get in touch with Rosenblum if anything turned up.

Rosenblum explained that if 'C' had not heard from him for a year it had been because he had had to acquire money and a proper background. He pointed to his recently acquired British wife and flat in Westminster.

He complained that Secret Service pay was too meagre to enable him to undertake intelligence work really successfully. He now had ample private means. Finally, he told 'C' there was no danger that his wife might indulge in careless talk as he had a hold over her such as few men had ever had over any woman.

'C' hesitated. Who was this strange young man who had emerged from the jungle of Brazil, spoke seven languages and seemed to know Europe like the palm of his hand? He did not even know his real nationality. He knew only that he was an expert pistol shot and was born in Russia – and even of the latter he had no proof. There was something decidedly sinister about this agent who refused to discuss his origins and past and who took leave when he decided. Whereas most agents worked for money, Rosenblum had acquired private means in order to be able to afford to work for him! And yet, the man had all the attributes of a first-class spy. Even if there was some risk in employing him, he could not afford to pass up the chance.

Rosenblum was back in the spy business and to mark the occasion he changed his name to Reilly, his wife's second name. He explained to 'C', who provided a new passport for him in the name of Reilly, that few people would completely trust anyone with a Jewish name and that with an Irish name such as Reilly he could, at times, if it was helpful in his work as an agent, make out that he was anti-British.

Thus, in 1899, was born Sidney Reilly, destined to become known the world over as Britain's master spy. Contrary to numerous newspaper reports, there was not a drop of Irish blood in his veins.

*   *   *

The spying career of Sidney Reilly now began in earnest and in a short time, he established himself as one of 'C's' most competent agents, if also the most unusual. He undertook a number of assignments abroad, the exact nature of which are not known but which are believed to have been relatively unimportant. There were days too of idleness with Margaret, while he awaited orders. At these times, whenever he returned to London, either to report to his chief or on completion of a mission, the money would flow. He spent much on clothes, more on his growing collection of Napoleana and more still at cards.

The Boer War found Reilly in Holland, passing himself off as a German and spying on Dutch aid to South Africa. Dutch was not one of the many languages he spoke. Moreover, the assignment had no connection with Russia – always his prime interest – and there was little scope for the dramatic. He was more than pleased when he was recalled to London in 1902 and asked by 'C' to go to Persia.

In the late nineteenth century, Ludwig and Robert Nobel, of the famous Nobel Prize family of Sweden, had been developing the oil resources of the Caucasus. Around the site of a temple of Zoroaster – the place of worship of an ancient cult of fire-worshippers – grew the now famous Baku oilfields of Russia.

In neighbouring Persia, where the geological formations were similar, exploration for oil had begun. In the U.S.A., oil had already been discovered in quantity; the Rockefeller oil empire was booming. Various discerning men in Europe, who foresaw a world dominated by oil, cast covetous eyes on Persia. Of the Great Powers, Great Britain, France and Russia were the most interested.

Early French efforts at exploration in Persia had either failed or been dropped as a result of Russian diplomatic pressure in Teheran. Russia had discovered oil within her own territory but had no particular wish to see any of the other Great Powers active across the Russian border in Persia. In 1901, however, William Knox D'Arcy, who had made a fortune founding the Mount Morgan Gold Mine of Australia, persuaded the Shah of Persia, in return for £10,000 cash, to grant him sole concession rights of oil exploration over most of Persia. The British Government was concerned about possible diplomatic reactions from Russia. The oil-minded gentlemen at the Admiralty wanted to know if and when oil in any quantity was likely to be discovered in Persia. The head of the British Secret Service was asked to make a report. Reilly, with his Russian background, seemed to 'C' to be the most suitable of his agents for the assignment.

'C' had once again to assure Reilly that the assignment did not involve him in action against the Russians. On the contrary, the British Government had no wish to antagonize Russia. Reilly's job was to discover the truth from the rumours which seethed in Teheran and to advise what action, if any, the British Government should take to prevent trouble with St. Petersburg. Many reports were reaching the Foreign Office from Embassies and Legations abroad, but Reilly's investigation was to be an entirely independent one.

Reilly, therefore, set out for the land of the Shah, the 'King of Kings, Master of Air, Land and Water, whose empire begins where the moon rises and ends in the fathomless depths of the sea'. As his cover, he adopted the role of manufacturer of patent medicines, cheap

c“urealls for the subjects of Shah Mozaffer-ed-Deen. In
fact, the Shah’s domain was scarcely an empire. Much
of the real power lay with the tribal chiefs. The country
was a barren plateau with hardly a road through it; it
was plagued by smallpox and so hot that the tempera-
ture reached 110 degrees in the shade by seven a.m.

On the back of a camel, the purveyor of patent
medicines rode the desert track to Chia Surkh where
Reynolds, D’Arcy’s chief lieutenant, had just begun
drilling. Reilly probed and questioned Reynolds and
his colleagues with an acute awareness of the problems
involved. He was soon satisfied that the men to whom
he spoke knew their business, that the geological
conditions were such that sooner or later they must
strike oil. Like D’Arcy, he foresaw the tremendous
consequences to the world if oil were discovered.
Equally important, he saw that despite the intolerable
conditions under which Reynold’s men worked, beset
by locusts, sunstroke, smallpox and a shortage of
water, they were firmly convinced that they could find
oil and were utterly determined they would.

In Teheran, Reilly obtained orders for his patent
medicines. He entertained and was received in the
home of the Atabeeg, or Grand Vizier. His charm
quickly found him friends in the Embassies and
Legations of the Persian capital. A witty conversationalist on almost any subject, he loosened many tongues.
He pretended to mock the ‘madmen’ drilling for oil at
Chia Surkh, but his seemingly innocent questions
about the possibility of finding oil and about the
potential interest in oil of the various Chanceries were
shrewd.

He left Teheran in a welter of goodwill. On his
return to England, he saw to it that the orders for

medicines which he had received were executed, subsidized out of his own pocket. The importers in Teheran were disappointed later when repeat orders could not be accepted!

To 'C', Reilly explained how the discovery of oil in Persia would revolutionize Britain and the world. The riches it could bring to Britain would make the treasures of the Arabian Nights pale into insignificance. Striding up and down 'C's' office, gesticulating with his hands, a trait which was always to reveal his Jewish blood in moments of excitement, Reilly insisted that the British Government should buy D'Arcy's concession as a matter of urgency.

He argued forcibly that there was no need to worry about the Russians. His soundings had shown that Russia would raise no objection provided Britain let her have her own way in the northern provinces of Persia. He asked for an agreement with Russia who was ready and waiting. He suggested Persia be divided up between Britain and Russia. He was adamant that oil would be found and spoke of the dawn of a magnificent new era. Reilly saw it as the starting-point of a great new alliance between Britain and Russia who, between them, could dominate the world!

The British Government carefully noted Reilly's report and took no action. The report, however, was not forgotten by some people and was to have a dramatic sequel a few years later. Meanwhile there were other jobs for Reilly.

Russia had leased the Liaotung Peninsula from the Chinese and was converting it into an important naval base. 'C' wanted detailed and continuous reports. Although it was tantamount to spying on his own

39

country, Reilly accepted the new assignment. With 'C's' permission, Margaret accompanied him. During Reilly's frequent absences 'on business' abroad, Margaret had taken to drinking and Reilly hoped that a trip to China and the resumption of a normal married life would cure her of the habit.

In Shanghai, Reilly obtained a quite humble post in a Russian shipping concern called the Compagne Est-Asiatique. In just six weeks he not only made his superior capabilities very evident to his bosses but persuaded them to appoint him the company's manager at Port Arthur.

In Port Arthur, the Russians were fortifying the new base at tremendous pace. The great armament firms of the world, Schneider, Krupp's, Blohm & Voss, sent representatives to supervise the installation of defences. From such men as these Reilly obtained many scraps of technical information. These scraps put together helped to build up an overall picture. The port teemed with Russian counter-espionage agents but Reilly successfully suborned a naval draughtsman and through him 'borrowed' a succession of plans which, in his office after hours, he would lay on a table between two sheets of glass and carefully photograph.

His life, however, was not free of problems. Margaret was still drinking heavily and behaving hysterically. There were violent quarrels. In addition, tension was mounting between Japan and Russia and, when an Anglo–Japanese alliance was concluded in 1902, Reilly was worried that his reports to London would be passed on to Japan – Russia's potential enemy.* Feeling that both his work and marriage were in jeopardy he made some drastic decisions. He sent Margaret back

* The Russo–Japanese war broke out on February 5th, 1904.

to Europe and, as he had done once before, reported to 'C', to the latter's fury, that he was taking indefinite leave.

For the best part of the next year, Reilly roamed the interior of China. It was a period in his life about which he always remained particularly secretive. It is known that he formed a deep attachment to a Chinese sage, Tzo-Lim, an enormous Manchu who introduced him to the various religious teachings of China. It was as if Reilly's soul needed refreshing for the bigger tasks that lay ahead. In later years, he would sometimes quote one of Tzo-Lim's favourite sayings: 'That which is escaped now, is but pain yet to come.' It was Tzo-Lim also who said to him: 'In each generation men are born with an especial capacity to lead or influence. I firmly believe that you are such a man.'

In the province of Shen-Si, Reilly spent some time in a lamaserie within the shadow of the Great Wall of China. The son of Israel, who had been brought up a Catholic, emerged a Buddhist. Many years later, his colleagues in the Secret Service used to jocularly address him as: 'O, Fortieth Re-incarnation of Buddha!'

Despite the inner tranquility which he had found in China under the guidance of Tzo-Lim, Reilly returned to London. On reaching England, Reilly found that Margaret had disappeared a year earlier having first withdrawn all the funds in their joint bank account. His hold over her had not been as strong as he had believed. All his enquiries led nowhere. The lady had vanished without trace and, apart from personal belongings in store, which included his collection of Napoleana, his only asset was a few hundred pounds' back pay which had been paid into his account after Margaret's disappearance.

With some difficulty he made peace again with 'C' after his period of 'French leave'. Reilly, however, was too good an agent to let go. During his absence in the Far East, the presence of oil in Persia had been proved – although admittedly in very limited quantities. Reilly asked to be sent back to Persia, but the realization of his dream to capture a vast oil empire for Britain had to await another year. In the meantime he was assigned to another mission – in Germany.

Under Kaiser Wilhelm II, the German armed forces were expanding as were the armaments factories. 'C' had managed to place an agent in the Krupp's works but no sooner had he started to send reports back to London than he had mysteriously disappeared; it was believed the Germans had discovered him and silently disposed of him. A replacement was urgently needed.

After a few weeks' apprenticeship in a Sheffield firm as a welder, Reilly set forth for Germany with cropped hair, roughened grimy hands, shabby clothes and worn boots. He was Karl Hahn, a German-Balt, from Reval, but a Russian subject who had been employed as a welder in the Putiloff shipyards of St. Petersburg.

Krupp's labour force was expanding and Reilly had little difficulty in getting signed on as a welder. His hours were long and the work was hard. Although he saw that additional workshops had recently been completed and several more were under construction, to obtain plans of these and details of the plant to be housed in them would not be easy. There seemed to be guards or watchmen everywhere and to stray from his own assembly line would at once arouse suspicion. The problem was solved when a factory notice appeared calling for volunteers for the works' fire-brigade. Night-shifts were involved and the fire-brigade crew would be called on to patrol the whole works. Reilly joined the fire-brigade.

Able to move more or less freely around the factory at night, Reilly, with the aid of pick-locks he had brought from England and a dimmed torch, made several raids on the Krupp's drawing office. In the plan-chests and on the drawing boards there were many plans and it took him some time to sort out those likely to be of most interest to 'C'. It was not practical to photograph them in the dark and he dared not 'borrow' them to copy in his lodgings. By torchlight he tried copying the plans on to tracing paper. This was not only difficult but involved far too much time. Freedom to move about as a member of the fire brigade was one thing but he could not disappear for hours on end into the drawing office each time he was on night shift. Reilly then hit on a brilliant idea. He persuaded the foreman in charge of the fire-brigade that a complete set of plans of the Krupp's works was needed to indicate the position of all fire-extinguishers and hydrants. The plans were soon produced and lodged in the foreman's office where all members of the works' fire-brigade could consult them.

It had been Reilly's intention to memorize the plans, section by section, and make drawings of them in the seclusion of his lodgings. Unfortunately, his rather frequent requests to the foreman for a sight of the plans aroused suspicions. Although he cleared himself in the face of some clumsy questioning from members of the Krupp's management and local police, he saw quite clearly that his time at Krupp's was nearly up. Reilly had only one course of action – to steal the plans and vanish.

Two days later, Reilly bought a train ticket to Dortmund and checked the time of the last train out of

Essen. Dortmund was twenty miles away and there, in the flat of one of 'C's' contacts, lay clothes, money and a new passport. Reilly had a key to the flat in case the contact was out; nothing was left to chance. He stamped and addressed four large envelopes; one addressed to London, the others to Paris, Brussels and Rotterdam. These he concealed in his clothing. He bought some leather reins from a local saddler and filled the pockets of his overalls with handkerchiefs and strips of sheet torn from his bed.

It was not as easy to surprise the foreman that night as Reilly had thought. Reilly had to throttle him to prevent him shouting and giving the alarm, but the fight was short. The now motionless German was rapidly bound and gagged; he might be dead but it was better to be on the safe side. Reilly drew out the plans from the desk, tore them into a number of large pieces which he put into the four stamped envelopes. If one letter went astray, the greater part of the plans would be in the other three.

On the way out of the factory, Reilly had to again adopt strong-arm tactics with a man on the gate. He too was bound and gagged and then dumped out of sight behind a pile of scrap metal.

Reilly posted his envelopes in a letter-box near the Essen station. It would be less important now if he himself were caught, but before the hue and cry could be raised he was on his way to Dortmund. The next day in a Savile Row suit and with a British passport, Reilly was *en route* to Paris. At the German frontier no-one was suspicious of the well-dressed Englishman carrying a smart leather suitcase.

* * *

Having sent a report to 'C', Reilly remained in Paris for a few days, enjoying the clean spring air and even more, after the grime and dirt of Krupp's, the luxury of a clean bedroom in his hotel in the Rue de la Paix, the feel against his skin of a hand-made silk shirt and the scent of a flower in his buttonhole. He was not the rich man he had been, but he was still young and there were plenty of desirable women in Paris.

At this point Fate dealt Reilly a cruel blow. Pausing one morning at a shop window in the Rue St. Honoré, he looked up at an attractive woman coming out of the shop. It was his half-sister Anna!

Following the death of her mother and the 'loss' of her half-brother, Anna had become more and more introspective and suffered long periods of morbid depression. She had learnt to play the piano as a child and had finally taken up music seriously. She had studied in Vienna and Warsaw and had come to Paris at the behest of the great Paderewsky, who had been impressed with her virtuosity. Recently, a Polish officer had fallen in love with her, followed her to Paris and had asked her to marry him. She did not love him but he was kind and she had just accepted.

Whether or not it was due to the shock of seeing her brother again no-one will ever know, but within a few days of the reunion Anna committed suicide by throwing herself out of the window of the top-floor bedroom of her Paris hotel. In a note left for 'Georgi' she said that she could not, after all, marry a man she did not love. Rather than face telling him, she preferred to end her life.

A grim and shattered Reilly stayed long enough in Paris to pull various strings so that a verdict of 'death by misadventure' was brought in at the inquest.

Anna's suicide left Reilly depressed and bitter. He experienced the torture known only to those who have mourned a suicide. The only two people he had ever really loved were both dead. The mother, who had 'betrayed' him and now Anna. It was ironic that he should have cut himself off from Anna by faking suicide. Had he not been so stubborn years ago, perhaps he would have kept in touch with Anna and somehow prevented this tragedy. Reilly dismissed this unprofitable speculation. Life had to go on. The bitterness, however, remained and although the worst of his depression lifted, the transient shadow of each woman that passed in the street troubled his memory.

On his return to London, Reilly was warmly congratulated by 'C' on his work in Germany. He usually thrived on such praise but this time the congratulations went unappreciated. Nor did the prospect of a couple of months' leave excite him. He drew his back pay, took rooms in St. James's and devoted himself to gambling and whoring in the West End. He made no attempt to seek news of Margaret.

IV

The Mede is at his gate!
The Persian on his throne!

BYRON

In 1904, Admiral Lord Fisher had become First Sea
Lord. Violent arguments now raged across the Admiralty boardroom table on the merits of oil as a fuel
for warships instead of coal. Fisher, known as the 'oil
maniac', was all for oil and to push forward his ideas
had set up an Oil Committee under the chairmanship
of the Civil Lord of the Admiralty. The U.S.A. had oil
in abundance but Britain had none – an intolerable
situation. D'Arcy's team had finally struck oil in
Persia both in 1903 and 1904 but not in commercial
quantities; the wells had run dry. D'Arcy had sunk
£225,000 of his personal fortune in Persia with no
return; his shares in Mount Morgan Mining were
pledged to the bank. British financiers, including Sir
Ernest Cassells and Joseph Lyons & Co., had refused
to back him. Desperate for more capital, D'Arcy was in
Europe trying to negotiate with foreign bankers for
additional finance.

This was the background to the new assignment
which 'C' gave Reilly one day early in 1905. The Royal
Navy had to have oil and Persia appeared the best,

indeed the only hope for oil supplies in quantity. The Oil Committee was seeking extra finance for D'Arcy. It was Reilly's task to see that if D'Arcy did sell out, it would be to Britain and to no-one else.

Reilly remembered how, several years earlier, he had urged that the British Government take over the D'Arcy concession. He wondered why the British were always so slow and unimaginative. He considered the position of Russia and asked himself whether, should D'Arcy plan a deal with Russia, he was meant to stop that too. He was angry that the British had not yet come to an agreement with Russia over Persia, as he had suggested long ago.

'C' assured him that there was no question of D'Arcy dealing with the Russians. He was negotiating with the French. 'C' also told Reilly that the Cabinet was at that moment considering the possibility of coming to an agreement with Russia and that his earlier recommendation had not fallen on entirely deaf ears.*

Reilly was briefed to be extremely circumspect in his approach to D'Arcy. If the French got wind of British anxieties that D'Arcy might sell out to them and learnt that an agent from London had been sent to France to prevent this, then it was certain that even if French private banks did not complete a deal with D'Arcy, the French Government would step in.

Reilly crossed over to Paris where he learnt that D'Arcy had indeed come to France and was negotiating with the Rothschilds. But in Paris itself there was no trace of D'Arcy. It was said that the French Rothschilds were

* In fact the Anglo–Russian Entente was not signed until August, 1907.

48

much interested in the oil concession and that secret talks were taking place in the South of France.

Reilly welcomed the idea of pitting his wits against the leaders of the Jewish banking world. In this, his first foray into big business, he was determined that he, the half-Jew, would get the better of the wholly Jewish Rothschilds.

His fertile imagination visualized a big financial reward from the British Government for saving the D'Arcy oil concession. He saw the British handing over to Russia the concessionary areas in north Persia. Russia, too, would be grateful. The Emperor himself would congratulate the illegitimate son of a Jew.

Coming down from his island of dreams to the mainland of reality, Reilly undertook a curious shopping expedition in Paris for his 'sick brother', boarded a train at the Gare de Lyon and stepped out on to the platform at Nice, swathed in the long black cloak of a French *curé*. For a stranger to approach D'Arcy when he was under the eye of the Rothschilds might give rise to questions but no-one would suspect a French priest of being an agent of the British Secret Service.

At his hotel in Nice, Reilly informed the staff that although he was on holiday he none the less hoped to approach some of the wealthy visitors to the South of France for a donation to a resettlement scheme for orphans in which he was interested. He mentioned the Rothschilds who were said to be then on the Riviera. No matter if they were Jews – his scheme was for orphans of any faith or none.

Almost immediately, Reilly learnt that there was indeed a gathering of the Rothschild family at Cannes where they maintained a large yacht. Leaving Nice, he moved into a small pension in Cannes and soon made his way down to the water's edge where he gazed with seemingly innocent curiosity at the various yachts. For two days he watched the comings and goings aboard the Rothschild yacht which lay alongside. From photographs he had seen in London he recognized D'Arcy's avuncular figure among those on board, but the financier never came ashore. Apparently he was sleeping on board the yacht.

Realizing that time was important and that D'Arcy might sign a deal with the Rothschilds at any moment, Reilly decided to act immediately. He boldly boarded the yacht as D'Arcy and his companions walked the deck.

Reilly was nothing if not voluble. A continuous stream of French cascaded from the lips of the *curé* as, waving his arms, he made a heartfelt appeal for funds for his orphanage. Those on board were at first speechless with surprise, but an animated discussion soon broke out on the merits, or otherwise, of giving the eccentric *curé* a donation.

Approaching D'Arcy, who could only guess at the subject of this conversation in French, Reilly took him by the arm and walked him to one side. When out of immediate earshot of the others, Reilly reverted to English, and, in quiet undertones, told D'Arcy that he had a message for him from the British Government. He said that the Admiralty would pay double anything the Rothschilds could offer for the oil concession and asked D'Arcy to meet him that evening for an apéritif at the Grand Hotel.* He suggested that the Englishman should tell the Rothschilds, as an excuse for leaving

---

* Situated on the Croisette, the Grand Hotel was the leading hotel in Cannes at that time.

the yacht, that he was very interested in the *curé's* orphanage and wished to discuss it further.

Before leaving the yacht, Reilly collected some quite handsome donations from the French bankers. In later years he would laugh at the good use to which these were put by the *curé's* favourite charity – Reilly himself!

At the Grand Hotel that evening, Reilly gave D'Arcy full details of the new interest in oil at long last aroused in Whitehall. He gave D'Arcy an assurance that even if the Admiralty might not pay as much as double any Rothschild offer it was certainly working on a scheme which would relieve him of all further financial worry. D'Arcy, still astounded by the approach made by Reilly aboard the yacht, could hardly believe what he heard. He nevertheless promised to stall for ten days and to sign nothing with the Rothschilds, provided Reilly obtained confirmation for him in writing of the Admiralty offer.

Thirty-six hours later Reilly was back in London reporting to 'C' that he had successfully prevented D'Arcy from making a deal with the Rothschilds. An immediate written offer from the British was essential.

The next day, the Rt. Hon. E. G. Pretyman, M.P., Civil Lord of the Admiralty, sent D'Arcy a letter asking him to suspend his discussions with the Rothschilds and inviting him to London for urgent negotiations with the Oil Committee. D'Arcy came home and on May 5th, 1905, as a result of Admiralty initiative, a Concession Syndicate was formed with the necessary finance and with the assistance of the Burmah Oil Company to continue exploration for oil in Persia. D'Arcy's interests in the event of oil being found were protected. Reilly had triumphed over the Roths-childs!

The benefits which Britain derived from this deal have proved incalculable.

At four a.m. on May 26th, 1908 the developers struck oil. This time the well did not dry up. From that day and hour, out of the once barren plains of Persia, oil has been gushing forth in abundance ever since – oil which has revolutionized life throughout the world; oil for ships, cars, aeroplanes and machines. Today, oil companies throughout the world spend no less than £4,000 million per annum on expanding their in-dustry.

In 1909 the concessionaires formed the Anglo-Persian Oil Company in which later, in 1914, on the recom-mendation of Winston Churchill, the British Govern-ment acquired a fifty-one per cent interest – an interest which it still holds in 1967. To millions throughout the world the company is today known under its present name of the British Petroleum Co. Ltd., or more simply 'B.P.'

Reilly never received the massive reward for which he had hoped nor any congratulations from the Tsar although he was, as usual, commended by 'C' for successfully completing another assignment. Perhaps he had only been a messenger, but what might have been the consequences to Britain had he failed to deliver the message in time? A man of lesser resource might not have boarded the Rothschild yacht until it was too late!

Reilly's old bitterness returned – a bitterness which flamed again both in 1907 when the Anglo–Russian

Entente was signed and in 1914 when the British Government acquired a direct interest in the Persian oilfields, a move which was considered as farsighted as Disraeli's purchase of the Suez Canal. Every step Reilly had urged years earlier had been taken. Except for 'C's' congratulations, there had been no recognition. The rewards of the successful secret agent are indeed intangible.

D'Arcy, on the other hand, was repaid all his earlier cash outlay and given £900,000 worth of Burmah Oil shares. A director of Anglo-Persian, he died in 1917 an exceedingly rich man.

Author's Note

In the early 1930's a widely circulated and quite untrue story began to appear in books and in the press both in Europe and in America that D'Arcy, having found oil in Persia, had gone insane with the excitement and become a religious maniac. It was said that Reilly, disguised as a priest, had followed D'Arcy around the world, become his father confessor and persuaded him to part with his concession in the belief that profits would go to religious charities. At the time this story was circulating, the Anglo-Persian Oil Company was engaged in delicate negotiations with the Shah of Persia for a new concession. In official quarters it was thought that this wildly distorted story had deliberately been put out by the French Foreign Office in order to discredit the British in the hope that the Shah would not grant them a new concession.

Great Britain was less prescient in the matter of the Saudi-Arabian oilfields. This concession might also have been Britain's for the gift of £20,000 in sovereigns to King Ibn Saud, but the Treasury refused the necessary exchange control permit. The concession went instead to Standard Oil of California and the Saudi-Arabian oilfields now export more than fifty million tons of oil per year.

V

The lucrative business of mystery.

EDMUND BURKE

Embittered by the death of Anna and the absence of any substantial reward for the D'Arcy assignment, Reilly decided to quit. An added factor in his decision was his pressing need of money, which for him was first and foremost a means to power as well as a prerequisite for the luxuries he loved. He decided that temporarily he must enter business.

Reilly rated himself a qualified chemist and, with influential contacts in many quarters, he had little difficulty in borrowing sufficient money to launch a patent medicine enterprise. Having, at this stage in his life, no first-hand knowledge of the United States, he took into partnership a young American named Long. From America, where the patent medicine racket was booming, Long was to bring over successful formulas: rheumatism cures, hair-restorers and pills to heal everything. These were to be made up in England and, in addition to selling patent medicines to a gullible British public, Reilly, with his European expertise, was to peddle pills in great quantities on the Continent.

Severed now from the world of politics and power which in recent years had been his stalking ground,

Reilly's inferiority complex returned. Once again he cursed his mother, his father and the whole Jewish race for his lot. There is a type of Jew who will abandon an obviously Jewish name to take another but Reilly did precisely the opposite. Through some perverse emotional impulse he reverted to the name of Rosenblum – the name which symbolized everything he hated.

Reilly's rooms in Cursitor Street were converted into offices and from here was launched the firm of Rosenblum & Long, Manufacturers of Patent Medicines. Despite his inexhaustible energy and enthusiasm, Reilly was something of an innocent in the world of business. The career of Rosenblum & Long was a chequered one for, although sales were good, the firm was constantly running foul of its customers on account of the unwarranted powers claimed for its products. There were costly breach of patent claims and Reilly was forced to borrow more money to keep the business afloat. After four unprofitable years Long absconded with the last £600 in the bank. It was perhaps a fitting conclusion to an unsatisfactory chapter in Reilly's life. Although under different circumstances Reilly was later to make a great deal of money, throughout his life he was inclined to trust others too easily in money matters – a strange contradiction in a man whose very life as a secret agent depended so often and so completely on dealing only with those whom he could trust.

Reilly's credit had run out and he was desperate for money. He obtained unexpected help from a certain Mr. Abrahams, the solicitor of one of his creditors. Mr. Abrahams took pity on the 'innocent' Reilly and although the latter was at first suspicious and loath to accept help from a Jew, he eventually allowed the

56

lawyer to sort out his affairs. Abrahams wound up the business for him, paid off the creditors and, to Reilly's astonishment, produced a final credit balance of some £160. Abrahams made no charge for his services and Reilly's opinion of his father's race underwent a profound change. After the Rosenblum & Long débacle he re-assumed the name of Reilly but in the years that followed he was to make many Jewish friends.

After the failure of his patent medicine business, Reilly's thoughts turned in an entirely different direction, toward the new wonder of the age – aviation. Just as his imagination had been fired by the possibilities of oil, so had it been kindled by the development of the aeroplane. In his various excursions to Paris on behalf of Rosenblum & Long, he had always found time to spend a few hours at the airfield and around the hangars of Farman, Blériot, Santos Dumont and other pioneers.

In 1910 when his business had been wound up and with nothing particular in mind except a feeling that something would turn up, Reilly went to Frankfurt to attend an international flying exhibition. Here he forgot the problem of his future as he watched the aerobatics and mingled with the pilots, engrossed by the new jargon of airmen. The pilots conversed freely with the man who had such a natural gift for making friends and who spoke so convincingly of plans to promote flying exhibitions in all the capitals of Europe. To Reilly, these men were his new gods, ranking only a little below Napoleon – the pioneers of a new era.

A god, however, was not quite the term to apply to

one pilot, a Welshman named Jones, who appeared to be a complete buffoon. Although he was said to have flown brilliantly at other exhibitions, he had made almost a beginner's crash-landing on the first day of the Frankfurt meeting. Now, without a plane, he seemed to spend most of his time idling in the hangars, telling jokes and occasionally helping the mechanics.

On the fifth day of the meeting a tragedy occurred; a German plane stalled, went into a spin and nose-dived straight into the airfield. Reilly, with a number of others, including pilots and mechanics, dashed to the scene of the crash. The pilot was dead, the plane a twisted ruin and Jones, one of the first to reach the wreck, seemed to have taken charge. He was directing pilots and mechanics in the task of dismantling and salvaging as much as possible of the wreck. Tools and trolleys were fetched and bits and pieces carted back to the hangars. Jones himself was concentrating on the engine and asked Reilly to give him a helping hand. Soon they cleared the engine from the mass of splintered spars, struts and torn fabric and with the help of some mechanics loaded it on to a trolly. Reilly noticed that Jones, for some reason, had covered the engine with a tail-plane. He turned to Reilly and asked him to assist in wheeling it back to his hangar. Speaking in an undertone and without his usual Welsh inflection, Jones said it was vital that he should have the engine to himself for five minutes. He spoke with commanding insistence and with no trace of buffoonery.

While crossing the airfield, Jones explained that he wanted secretly to remove the magneto and substitute a replacement. He asked Reilly to assist by diverting the attention of any onlookers.

Questions were unnecessary. Reilly's intuition had not failed; something had turned up.

The task of changing the magneto was quickly completed. Later, Jones made rapid but detailed drawings of the German magneto and, when the engine had been removed to its rightful place in the hangar of the German pilots, Jones and Reilly managed to switch the magnetos once again, restoring the original. The German pilot who had been killed had boasted to Jones of his new magneto; the German army were interested, as it was far ahead of other designs. Having examined it, Jones was satisfied that the young German's claim was true.

Reilly was astonished not so much by Jones's behaviour as by the fact that he should know all about him – Reilly! Jones – and his name *was* Jones, or so he said – was in reality an engineer commander in the Royal Navy and had been working for 'C' for some time.

In Frankfurt, Reilly and Jones talked at great length of the coming of the air age and of the likelihood of war with Germany. Germany was building a navy to fight Britain's. Reilly felt some satisfaction at the thought that if war came Russia and Britain would probably fight alongside each other.

It was Jones who suggested to Reilly that he work for 'C' again. He knew that 'C' would welcome him back.

Once more, Reilly rejoined the S.I.S. His assignment was Russia. 'C' gave him a completely free hand. He was to be completely on his own; even the British Ambassador would be unaware of his mission. The

Secret Service, as usual in time of peace, was short of funds and Reilly, although almost broke, was too proud to accept the meagre salary offered by 'C'. Instead he took a 'float' of £600 for expenses to set himself up in St. Petersburg and declared that he would easily find a cover job which would make him self-sufficient. His assignment was not to spy on Russia but to collect, through Russian sources, all the intelligence he could on German military and naval power. War seemed increasingly probable and every scrap of information about Germany's strength and intentions was vital.

Reilly arrived in St. Petersburg with no firm ideas other than to organize an international air meeting in Russia, to which the Germans would be invited. The publicity involved would quickly establish him in St. Petersburg society and such a meeting would bring him into contact with German aviators who, for the most part, had connections with the German army.

On the day of his arrival in St. Petersburg, Reilly went down the Morskaya* to Kuba's restaurant for lunch. Kuba's, whose praises have been sung by Pushkin, was, in the days of the Tsar, one of the most famous eating-places in Europe. Those who have had the good fortune to dine there have described the cuisine as the finest they have ever known – in or out of Russia. Decorated in the elaborate French style of the period, there were upholstered armchairs for every customer. In the kitchen, the chefs were French to a man. The waiters were all Tartars.

At Kuba's on his first day in St. Petersburg, Reilly ran into an old friend from his Port Arthur days. This

* One of the principal streets of St. Petersburg.

was Boris Souvorin, son of A. A. Souvorin, owner of *Novoe Vremya*, one of Russia's leading newspapers. Boris was becoming a well-known journalist himself. Something of a personality, he had married a popular gypsy singer, Valia Panina* and was a staunch anglophile. The man eating *zkooski*† at the table with Boris was Alexander Ivanovich Grammatikoff. Known as Sasha to his friends, Grammatikoff was a rising barrister. His ancestors, well-born Greeks, had migrated from Turkey to the Crimea at the invitation of Catherine the Great, after Crimea had been added to Russia's domains at the end of the eighteenth century. The population of the Crimea, for long under Turkish rule, was largely Muslim and Catherine was anxious to have Christians of sound stock to govern her new subjects. Among those invited from Turkey to fill these roles were Grammatikoff's forebears.

Reilly accepted Souvorin's invitation to join them. Sasha Grammatikoff, then a stranger to Reilly, was to become one of his closest friends. For several years the two men were to lunch at Kuba's almost daily, sitting at the same table and in the same chairs. Boris Souvorin was often to be their companion. Many times in later years, after the Russian Revolution had removed Kuba's from the gastronomic map, Reilly looked back wistfully on that first meeting. Grammatikoff's first impression of Reilly was that here was a man who, without revealing anything of himself, could hold his companions spell-bound with his conversation. After fifteen years of the closest friendship, to Grammatikoff he still remained a man of mystery.

* Valia Panina was well known in Paris between the two wars. In the 1930's she was suspected of being a Soviet agent.
† A Russian hors d'oeuvre.

Out of this meeting sprang a plan for an air race, by stages from St. Petersburg to Moscow, a distance of 390 miles. Reilly, Souvorin and Grammatikoff formed a flying club. It was called The Wings Aviation Club and became better known simply as 'Wings'. The club had no aircraft but neither had its only rival, the Imperial Aero Club. Reilly himself went to see Count Stenbok-Fermor, the President of the rival club, and won his support for a jointly sponsored flying week, to which foreign aviators would be invited. The climax was to be the flight from St. Petersburg to Moscow, restricted to Russian pilots.

Souvorin took care of newspaper publicity and together with Grammatikoff found sufficient financial support to make the event a considerable success. Of the ten pilots who set out from St. Petersburg for Moscow, only one, Vasilliev, finished, but Reilly was on the Hodinsky Field* to greet him. Reilly felt that at long last he had been of service to Russia.

Reilly's part in the St. Petersburg Flying Week established him firmly in St. Petersburg society and the news filtered back across Europe. To Margaret, who had been brooding these past years in Brussels, dissipating her money on drink, it seemed the right moment to reclaim her husband. He was apparently a successful man, and presumably rich as well. Her own funds were low and life in St. Petersburg sounded exciting. She arrived without warning.

Reilly was enraged by the reappearance of his wife. Margaret, however, held a strange power over him, derived perhaps from the circumstances of the death of

* Now the Moscow Air Terminal.

her first husband, and in St. Petersburg she stayed. With Reilly she set up a home in Potchtamsky Street. She continued to drink.

Margaret's presence in St. Petersburg, however, did not prevent Reilly from achieving his next triumph, one of the most brilliant in the history of espionage.

As cover for his clandestine activities, Reilly first obtained a post at the head office in St. Petersburg of his former employers, the Compagnie Est-Asiatique, for whom he brought off one or two important business deals. He rapidly built up a circle of useful contacts and consolidated his position in the Russian capital. Although always abstemious over food and drink, he was frequently to be seen in the best hotels and restaurants. Less abstemious when it came to women, he acquired several mistresses. Whereas for most spies women friends are potential sources of danger to whom secrets may be revealed in unguarded moments, for Reilly they formed part of his 'network' of agents. He combined business with pleasure and chose his mistresses exclusively from among those women who, on account of their husbands or their liaisons with other men, could provide him with valuable intelligence. He indulged in his one vice – gambling, usually playing at the Koupechesky Club* where the stakes were the highest in St. Petersburg.

Although Reilly generally knew when to stop if the cards went against him, he led a colleague in the Compagnie Est-Asiatique to suicide. Hoffman, the chief cashier of the company, in trying to emulate Reilly's panache at the gaming tables, lost more than

* Also known as the Merchants' Club.

he could afford, dipped into the firm's till and one day took a dose of cyanide at the Hotel d'Europe.

Within a few months of his return to Russia, Reilly was not only established in society and business but had also created for himself the image he desired. To his friends in St. Petersburg, he was, if something of a mystery, a man of business without any real national or political attachments, an Irishman but a cosmopolitan, whose recreations were women and cards. As in a game of chess, Reilly had first moved his pawns. He was now ready to bring his bigger pieces into play.

The Russian navy, destroyed in the Russian–Japanese war, was to be rebuilt. A five-year construction programme, approved by the Government and sanctioned by the Tsar, was coming into operation in 1911. A vast amount of money was to be spent. As the capacity of Russia's shipbuilding yards and armament factories was insufficient to handle more than a tenth of this programme, orders for the great majority of ships would have to be placed abroad. For these contracts, the great naval shipbuilders of the world were competing fiercely.

France, as Russia's ally, considered herself in a privileged position and the efforts of the French were channelled through their naval attaché – a man who had been in St. Petersburg for many years and who knew the price of every man who could be bribed. The British, the acknowledged leaders in naval construction, thought they should have the lion's share. The British firms worked independently, but the spearhead was Vickers with an army of agents under the leadership of Basil Zaharoff,* often called 'The mystery man

* Later Sir Basil Zaharoff, G.C.B., G.B.E.

of Europe'. The Germans, however, with their influence at the court of the Tsar and their extensive business connections in Russia, were likely to get most of the orders.

On all these matters, Reilly was well informed. He had made it his business to meet the hierarchy of the Russian Admiralty. He had become a close friend of the Naval Assistant to the Minister of Marine, and of his attractive wife Nadine Massino, and he was a frequent visitor at their house. It has been said of Reilly that when he chose to exercise his charm, there were few who could resist it. To the Russian naval officer and, even more, to his wife, Reilly was charm itself.

Reilly soon confirmed for himself that the bulk of the Russian naval construction orders would probably go to Germany. He learnt, too, that many of the contracts were likely to be placed with Blohm & Voss, the giant naval constructors of Hamburg. Blohm & Voss were about to appoint Russian agents in St. Petersburg for the purpose of handling tenders and Reilly found out that any such appointment would first have to be approved by the Minister of Marine. Among the firms the Germans were likely to appoint as agents was one by the name of Mendrochovich & Lubensky.

Reilly knew Mendrochovich and a brilliant plan began to take shape in his mind.

Mendrochovich & Lubensky was a relatively small company which had, none the less, prospered by selling German goods wagons to the Russian railways. Mendrochovich, a self-educated Jew who had been the brains of the business, was now an old man; Count Lubensky, who had been taken into the business as a contact man and because his name added cachet, had not lived up to Mendrochovich's expectations.

When Reilly learnt that Blohm & Voss had short-listed for Russian approval three firms as possible agents and that Mendrochovich & Lubensky was on the list, he produced a convincing argument to Nadine's husband that Mendrochovich's firm was the only one the Russians should consider. The naval assistant to the Minister of Marine, who in a short time had come to regard Reilly almost as an oracle on the St. Petersburg business community, was persuaded by him to put forward only one name to his Minister – that of Mendrochovich & Lubensky.

By *droshky** Reilly drove straight to Mendrochovich. He came at once to the point, asking the Jew what the Blohm & Voss agency was worth to him. Mendrochovich, or 'Mendro' as he was called by his friends, knew exactly what such an agency would mean. He knew too that Reilly had friends in the Ministry of Marine and realized that if he did not make a satisfactory offer, the agency might go elsewhere. He had to be generous.

He offered Reilly 200,000 roubles down and twenty-five per cent on the profits the business brought in.

Reilly asked for a fifty-fifty share on the profits and the bargain was struck. Within two weeks Mendrochovich & Lubensky received a letter from Blohm & Voss appointing them as sole agents for Russia. The appointment had been approved by the Minister of Marine.

As soon as Reilly heard the appointment had been made, he again called on Mendrochovich. He pointed out that whereas Mendrochovich had the agency he still needed the contracts. These and fantastic profits

* A Russian horse-drawn cab which plied for hire.

Reilly promised, provided he was himself taken into the firm. A second bargain was struck.

Reilly who was working entirely on his own for 'C' in Russia and was not in contact with any other British agent had meanwhile sent an urgent coded message to London. He asked for a senior man from S.I.S. headquarters to come immediately to St. Petersburg to discuss a most important plan he had devised. It was Jones who came.

Like many brilliant ideas, Reilly's plan was almost childlike in its simplicity. He was to work as the agent in Russia for Blohm & Voss. He knew exactly how to handle Mendrochovich; for all practical purposes he would control the business. His friends at the Ministry of Marine would ask to see all the designs of the newest German warships and of those not yet built. All the specifications and blueprints would pass through his hands.

Every single innovation in warship design for the German fleet, armour plating, guns, torpedoes, engines – the British could have them all. The only question was, would the British mind these large ship-building orders going to Germany instead of to Britain? Jones thought not, but promised to ask for an immediate decision on his return to London. They worked out methods of communication and of forwarding copies of the plans and discussed once again the question of Reilly's remuneration. Reilly said it was unnecessary for 'C' to pay him anything:

'I don't suppose "C" will mind if the Germans foot the bill! I should make a lot of money out of them.'

Soon after Jones had returned to London, Reilly received the go-ahead. He resigned from the Compagnie Est-Asiatique and joined Mendrochovich. For the next three years, he worked like a fanatic while Mendro sat back and gloated over the contracts for Blohm & Voss coming in from the Ministry of Marine. The Russian naval staff followed Reilly's persistent suggestions that it should press Blohm & Voss for later and still later designs, whether for a whole cruiser or for guns for some new destroyers. Plans for nearly all existing German warships were requested for comparison with the new designs.

At first, the Germans looked on Reilly with not unnatural suspicions. Their agents kept watch on both his flat and his office. However, as the contracts for Blohm & Voss kept on mounting and as he was so obviously working strenuously on Germany's behalf, the watchdogs were soon called off.

As Blohm & Voss obtained contract after contract, the British and French became more and more furious. Reilly was soon ostracized by the British community in St. Petersburg and representatives of British firms protested to the Ambassador at his disloyalty. The great French combine of Schneider Creusot was enraged and Basil Zaharoff came in person to Russia to see for himself 'that man Reilly' who was defeating the Vickers' agents at every turn. Zaharoff even tried to buy Reilly over to Vickers and was astonished when he turned down an offer for even more money than he was making out of the Blohm & Voss business. The Germans, on the other hand, were delighted with Reilly's work, but they would have been less pleased had they known that all their naval designs were going straight to London. Every set of plans was sent from Germany in a sealed envelope by diplomatic bag to the German Embassy in St. Petersburg; then the envelope, marked 'To be delivered to the appropriate authority of the Russian Ministry of Marine', went by hand to the office of Mendrochovich and Chubersky.* Every envelope was opened by Reilly.

Reilly worked behind locked doors in his flat in Potchtamsky Street. He took a cast of every seal he had to break and used a special steam press to open each envelope so as to leave no trace of tampering. He spent hours with a hot iron and layers of blotting paper, placing the blueprints between sheets of glass and making photostat copies. And there was always the fear that sooner or later someone would notice the consistently long intervals between the time he took the envelopes from his office for delivery to the Ministry of Marine and the time he actually handed them over.

His duplicity was completely successful. For three vital years before the outbreak of the First World War, the British Admiralty were kept up to date with every new design or modification in the German fleet – tonnages, speeds, armament, crew and every detail even down to cooking equipment.

Through an association with one of Rasputin's lady-friends, Reilly was also able to keep in close touch with court circles and passed on to Britain considerable political intelligence as well.

The big problem at this time was Margaret. Reilly's relationship with the Naval Assistant to the Minister of Marine had grown into something more than a business one. He wished to marry his wife Nadine. When Margaret refused Reilly's offer of £10,000 to divorce him, he gave her a forty-eight-hour ultimatum to accept. He made the alternative frighteningly clear and

* Once in control, Reilly soon replaced Count Lubensky with an able banker named Chubersky.

Margaret, knowing only too well that Reilly did not make idle threats, wisely caught the Vienna Express and fled the country.

Nadine's husband, on the other hand, was more amenable than Margaret; for a considerable sum of money he agreed to a divorce from Nadine. Reilly engaged Sasha Grammatikoff to handle the divorce but although Nadine would soon be free to remarry, Reilly himself might not be. Assiduous enquiries he had made showed that, from Vienna, Margaret had made her way via Belgrade to Sofia where, it was said, she had joined the International Red Cross. Reilly decided that if he could not kill Margaret one way, he would kill her another; his journalist friend, Boris Souvorin, would be his accomplice. And it was not long before a story, under the dateline Sofia, appeared in Souvorin's newspaper, *Novoe Vremya*, reporting the crash in Bulgaria of a Red Cross ambulance which had swerved off a mountain road and fallen into a ravine. Several nurses had been killed 'including a Mrs. Reilly who until recently was a resident of St. Petersburg'.

Nevertheless, Reilly still had to wait before he could marry Nadine. Her divorce took longer than expected and by early 1914, with the divorce still not completed, the threat of war in Europe was growing. To get her out of harm's way, Reilly sent Nadine to Nice. He intended to join her when war broke out, as he was sure it would, since German naval construction for Russia, which had already slackened off, would then obviously cease.

On August 1st, 1914, Germany declared war on Russia. It was a war in which Reilly, after a quiet start, played a dramatic role; a war in which his audacity and courage all but changed the course of history.

VI

Fortune aids the brave.

TERENCE

Two days after the outbreak of war, when Reilly's work for the British Secret Service was temporarily at an end, he received a very attractive proposition from the brothers Jivatovsky who controlled the Russo-Asiatic Bank. Impressed by Reilly's success as the Blohm & Voss agent, the Jivatovskys invited him to go first to Japan and thence to the U.S.A. as the bank's representative. Acting on behalf of the Russian Government, he was to buy raw materials which were urgently needed for the manufacture of high explosives, and other war supplies. Even Reilly was staggered by the salary and commission offered. He accepted without hesitation.

Two weeks later, with his friends Grammatikoff and Souvorin on the platform of the Nicolai station to see him off, Reilly left for Moscow to catch the Trans-Siberian Express. It was to be nearly four years before he was to see Russia again.

Reilly spent little time in Japan, which had few war supplies to spare, and he was soon established in New York, a city where the pace of life suited his temperament. There he began to buy munitions in competition with the Germans. Only months earlier he had been buying from the Germans and the knowledge of German purchasing methods he had acquired in Russia now stood him in good stead. He set up his own intelligence network and was soon familiar with the scope and methods of most German activities, both commercial and political, in the United States.

Reilly bought war supplies for Russia with singular efficiency. He was glad to be of service to his country and more than satisfied with the money he was making. The British had once again lost their best but most infuriating agent and Captain Mansfield Cumming, C.B., R.N., who was the new head of the S.I.S., or M.I.1C., as it was now called, instructed his agents in America not to lose touch with Reilly. Britain was at war and good spies were at a premium.

Sir William Wiseman, head of the British Purchasing Commission in the United States and Cumming's 'man in New York' together with Major Norman Thwaites, M.C.* another of 'C's' agents, pressed Reilly to rejoin the S.I.S. but he was very content with the work he was doing. He was quite willing to provide Sir William with the detailed intelligence he had amassed about German munitions' buying, but to resume full-time work for the British was out of the question. He had a job to do for Russia.

Later, when Germany, worried at the increasingly large quantities of war supplies the United States was sending to the Allies, set up sabotage units to blow up American factories, Reilly and his private corps of spies soon uncovered the German agents. He kept a close eye on the saboteurs and gave full details of their plans to

* Later Lieutenant-Colonel N. G. Thwaites, C.B.E., M.V.O., M.C.

Sir William Wiseman and to Thwaites. The British were delighted. Though they obviously did not want to see the destruction of war supplies destined for the Allied armies they had good reason to welcome German sabotage activity since this was certain to swing public opinion in the United States further towards entering the war. It is very doubtful whether the British passed to the American Government all the information which Reilly obtained about German sabotage plans.

Reilly was thoroughly enjoying his work. He was happy also to have Nadine with him, for, soon after his arrival in the United States, he had arranged for her to join him from the South of France. On her arrival in New York, she had been detained by the immigration authorities who suspected that Reilly was importing her for immoral purposes! She was soon released but Reilly deferred their marriage. Although he had told Nadine of Margaret's 'death', he privately still hoped to trace Margaret and either arrange a divorce or dispose of her by cruder methods. He made various excuses for postponing the marriage but Nadine eventually became impatient and in 1916 they were married in the Greek-Orthodox Cathedral in New York. Reilly described himself as a widower but was, in fact, a bigamist.

By the time of Reilly's marriage to Nadine, American public opinion was strongly on the side of the Allies and increasing numbers of Americans were joining the British or Canadian fighting services. The Canadian forces were making recruiting drives in the United States, whistle-stop tours with up and coming artistes who gave variety shows to pull in the crowds. One autumn day in 1916, to pass an idle hour, Reilly went to see a show staged in New York by the Royal Canadian Flying Corps. He was completely enthralled by the brilliant performance of a young dancer and his partner. On impulse, Reilly made a decision then and there – a decision which not only altered the whole pattern of his life but brought him to the climax of his career. The magic feet of Fred Astaire and his sister Adele had succeeded, where the blandishments of Sir William Wiseman and Major Thwaites had failed. Reilly had firmly decided he would take a direct and active part in the war.

Having made his decision Reilly went straight to Sir William Wiseman for advice. With Sir William's approval he enlisted in the Royal Canadian Flying Corps, in which, after a few months' training, it was certain he would be sent to England. Sir William arranged that on Reilly's arrival in England he would be transferred to M.I.1C. Thwaites had suggested there was nothing to stop Reilly going to England straightaway, but Reilly insisted on a few months' grace to build up for himself a background as a British flying officer. Always air-minded, the Royal Canadian Flying Corps was at hand – and he found the uniform attractive!

He wound up his business affairs, which infuriated the Jivatovsky brothers, and took leave of Nadine, whom he advised to remain in New York until the war was over. He then went to Toronto and enlisted in the R.C.F.C.

A few months later he found himself in England face to face with the fifty-seven-year-old Captain Mansfield Cumming. It was his first meeting with the new 'C', a square-built man with white hair and a wooden leg. He had a sharp wit, a gay disposition and an eye for a pretty girl. He was also a keen motorist who drove at great speed and had lost his leg in a motor crash. It was said that he had been pinned under his car and had had to cut off his leg with a pen-knife in order to free himself. Occasionally, when interviewing people in his office he would enjoy disconcerting them by taking a knife off his desk and sticking it into his wooden leg. He was a fanatical admirer of Gilbert and Sullivan. Devoted to his job, he was respected by all who worked for him. This was the man who was to be Reilly's boss in the ensuing years – although 'boss' is hardly the word anyone could have applied to a relationship with Reilly. To Cumming, Reilly was 'a man of indomitable courage, a genius as an agent but a sinister man whom I could never bring myself wholly to trust'.

Reilly arrived in England early in 1917 and was given the rank of captain in the Royal Canadian Flying Corps. During the next twelve months or more he was to undertake a series of missions into Germany, which for sheer audacity are unlikely to have been surpassed by any spy before or since.

The colleagues with whom Reilly worked during this period were different from those with whom he was associated both before and after. They are mostly dead or untraceable. The records of the Secret Service concerning Reilly's activities at this time are said to have been destroyed. Although he frequently boasted of what he hoped to do, Reilly was usually modest about his past achievements. Often he would quote an old Russian proverb; 'The cow that makes the most noise gives the least milk.' Of his work in Germany he was, on the whole, reticent.

In the years following the First World War, stories of Reilly's exploits gradually emerged – many from Germany itself. It was said that the German High

Command were more afraid of Reilly, the master spy, than of a whole army corps.

Some of the newspaper accounts of Reilly's missions to Germany, published in the 1920s and 1930s, were undoubtedly apocryphal but the truth was more fantastic than the fiction. Major Thomas Coulson, C.B.E., the author of a life of Mata Hari, made it clear that Germany's notorious spy was never in the same class as Reilly.

Reilly was dropped by plane many times behind the German lines; sometimes in Belgium, sometimes in Germany, sometimes disguised as a peasant, sometimes as a German officer or soldier, when he usually carried forged papers to indicate he had been wounded and was on sick-leave from the front. In this way he was able to move throughout Germany with complete freedom.

Once when walking through a Belgian village, dressed as a peasant, he was arrested on suspicion and brought before a German military court. Reilly posed as the village idiot and was released to continue gathering information on German troop movements while grinning inanely at the German soldiers who mocked him.

For a short period he took active service in the German army. Enlisting as a private, he was almost immediately promoted to commissioned rank. Every minute of the day he faced the possibility of exposure and the firing squad.

Not only did Reilly operate in central Germany and behind the Western Front but, according to his colleague Thwaites, he was also in East Prussia where, disguised as a German officer, he messed with German officers in Königsberg. With his flawless German and

Russian, he could pass equally well as a native of either country. He would cross through the German–Russian lines and report back information from both camps.

Of the various versions told of Reilly's meeting with the Kaiser, the story reconstructed in Chapter I is believed to be the true one. It was the one Reilly himself gave. At German headquarters, in the councils of the Imperial High Command, Reilly learnt of the plans for the massive U-boat onslaught on British shipping which nearly won the war for Germany in 1917. Thanks to him the British Admiralty were fore-warned.

There were often repeated newspaper accounts that Reilly, having obtained the position of a junior German staff officer, was chosen for his brilliance from among all the junior officers in the German army to discuss the overall war strategy alone with the Kaiser. These reports can be discounted; the true story is astonishing enough.

The story of Reilly's life would be more complete if detailed and official accounts of his missions in Germany could be made known. Here is surely a case for some relaxation of the Official Secrets Act; Reilly's amazing exploits in Germany for the Secret Intelligence Service took place fifty years ago. Even if the records have not been destroyed, it is unlikely that they will ever be made public. It seems we shall have to be satisfied with Thwaites' statement that much of the kudos reaped by other spies in reality belonged to Reilly.

It is perhaps appropriate that for posterity some mystery should still surround Reilly. His life after all was full of mystery.

Part Two

VII

Revolutions are not made with rose-water.

LORD LYTTON

Of all the events which shook the world in the First
World War, the most momentous was the Russian
Revolution. To grasp the full importance of Reilly's
next assignment, the greatest of his career, it is necessary to know the background of the turbulent events
which led up to Reilly's despatch by Lloyd George to
Moscow in 1918.

For centuries, the Tsars had ruled as despots and if
Nicolas II was a good deal less despotic than some of
his predecessors, he was no less autocratic. He had a
singular capacity for choosing the wrong advisers,
including the evil Rasputin, who dominated the hys-
terical Empress. He was totally out of touch with what
was happening in war-time Russia, which, by 1916,
was a war-weary country. His gallant but inadequately
equipped army was being mauled by the Germans
while in the cities and towns the people starved in the
bread queues. In Petrograd,* the aristocracy and rich
bourgeoisie continued to live an orgiastic existence in

* The name of the Russian capital was changed from St. Petersburg
to Petrograd in 1914.

which champagne, caviar and bedding their coach-mens' daughters and their neighbours' wives were the main ingredients. The Russian nobility was an intellectual superfluity lost in artificial life, in sensual pleasure and in unbroken egoism. They had reduced love for women to a kind of voracious gourmandise.

This situation could not last. To meet increasing protests and warnings from the more far-sighted Liberal politicians, the Emperor changed his ministers with bewildering rapidity, but to no avail. Each new minister was as ineffectual as his predecessor. The Social-Revolutionary Party began what amounted to revolutionist agitations.

On March 11th, 1917, rioting broke out in Petrograd and quickly spread to Moscow. On March 15th a new 'democratic' Government was formed, with Prince Lvoff at its head, comprised mainly of Liberals, Constitutional Monarchists and Social-Revolutionaries. The next day the Tsar abdicated. The body of Rasputin, who had been murdered a few months before was dug up and burnt.

On the whole it was a peaceful revolution and the war against the Germans continued. But, as a sinister portent of what was to come, Bolshevik newspapers began to appear on the streets. The future masters of Russia, who were living in exile abroad, began to pack their suitcases – ready to move in at the right moment.

Revolutionary and anti-war sentiment increased throughout Russia. The Social-Revolutionaries gained the upper hand and eventually it was Kerensky who held the reins of Government. But Kerensky for all his peaceful revolutionism, tried to keep Russia in the war. His was a vain hope and his Minister of War, Boris Savinkoff, the master of assassination plots, of whom a good deal more will be heard later, was always to regret that Kerensky had not been among those whose assassination he had ordered.

Discipline in the Russian army deteriorated. The soldiers not only lacked equipment, but were now as near famine as the mass of Russian people themselves. The military reverses continued; the bread queues in Moscow grew longer.

By September, 1917, the *droshky* horses were dropping dead from starvation in the streets of Petrograd. It was then that Lenin, lurking in Finland, moved swiftly and secretly into the Russian capital.

By the end of October, the Bolsheviks had decided to act. Soldiers were deserting from the front, murdering their officers as they went. Officers fortunate enough to escape murder were deprived of their rank and expelled from the army by committees of privates. The latter were controlled by the Military Revolutionary Committee of the Soviets, a Bolshevik and Menshevik organization.

When Kerensky outlawed the Military Revolutionary Committee, Lenin pounced from his headquarters at the Smolny Institute – formerly an aristocratic girls' school – with his clandestinely organized Red Guard of soldiers, sailors and workmen. By November 8th, Kerensky's Government was in flight and Lenin had seized Petrograd. Moscow was taken a few days later. The Soviet Government had come to power and Lenin's policy was to make peace with Germany.

In the months that followed, all was turmoil and chaos in Russia. Overnight, privates became generals and railway porters found themselves commissars. Bands of anarchists roamed both town and country, pillaging and murdering at will. Not only horses but men and children starved in the streets. Troops still loyal to Tsarist generals were fighting Bolshevik forces when they were not fighting Germans. The Social-Revolutionaries fought both. Although Lenin was determined on peace with the Germans, Trotsky had other ideas. A flamboyant character with his great mass of black, wavy hair and a long prominent nose, Trotsky fancied himself as a military commander and was, at first, all for continuing the war. It was a situation which the Germans exploited to the full.

In Britain and France there was bewilderment. The Allied Governments were convinced that the Bolshevik regime could not endure and that the old order would be restored. In London, at the Foreign Office, there was no-one who could even speak Russian. In the Cabinet Offices, Lord Carson,* who had never heard of a Marxist, asked what was the difference between a 'Marximalist' and a 'Bolshevik'!

With the exception of one or two military mission personnel and Secret Service agents who were primarily concerned with intelligence operations against Germany, Allied missions almost ceased to function. They were later either withdrawn or they retired in safety to Vologda, hundreds of miles from the seat of Soviet power.

In January, 1918, over the heads of the Foreign Secretary and the Foreign Office Chiefs, Lloyd George sent Bruce Lockhart, former Consul-General in Moscow, into this maelstrom as head of a special mission to establish relations with the Bolsheviks. His brief from Lloyd George was to keep Russia in the war.

* First Lord of the Admiralty in 1917 and Minister without portfolio in the War Cabinet, 1917–18.

Bruce Lockhart knew Russia and all sections of the Russian people well. He spoke fluent Russian. He quickly established friendly relations with the Bolshevik leaders and in particular with Trotsky, who was for maintaining the struggle against Germany. Bruce Lockhart was soon convinced that the one hope of preventing a separate peace and of stopping the Germans from exploiting the position was for the Allies to co-operate with the new Soviet Government. However, the British Government vacillated; the War Cabinet firmly believed that Lenin and Trotsky were German agents. As Trotsky himself said: 'Lloyd George is like a man playing roulette and scattering chips on every number.' Lenin was even more scathing when he described the British Prime Minister as 'a first-class bourgeois trickster and political card-sharper'.

By February, 1918, the military and economic situation in Russia was desperate and German troops were advancing towards Petrograd. In March, even a humiliated and furious Trotsky was forced to agree to the German peace terms imposed at Brest-Litovsk. In the same month, the Bolsheviks transferred their seat of Government to Moscow, which was geographically a more suitable capital though the Tsar had never liked it; his uncle, the Grand Duke Serge, had been blown to bits there by a bomb and hundreds had been trampled to death in the Moscow streets by troops at his own coronation.

Although the British and French Governments were convinced that the Bolshevik leaders were traitors and in the pay of the Germans, in reality the new masters of Russia had little alternative to making peace.

In London and Paris there were insistent demands

for Allied intervention. With Trotsky now Soviet Minister of War and pining to avenge Brest-Litovsk, there was still hope that Russia, with Allied help, would resume fighting. Intervention without Soviet agreement would force the Bolsheviks into the hands of the Germans, but Whitehall continued to ignore the warnings of Bruce Lockhart. Serious warnings from the French General Lavergne, who was in Moscow, were also ignored by Noulens, the French Ambassador, who, miles away in Vologda, said he would have no dealings with cut-throats.

In London, opinion hardened in favour of intervention. At all costs, the Bolsheviks must be made to resume fighting or be overthrown. Bruce Lockhart was labelled a pro-Bolshevik and nearly recalled. While plans for intervention were being prepared, something had to be done at once to expedite the fall of the Soviet Government.

This was the task of Sidney Reilly, code name 'S.T.1'.

Lloyd George consulted Cumming who realized that if any one man could organize the downfall of the Bolsheviks, that man was Reilly. However important his recent work in Germany had been, there was now a greater need. Cumming knew, too, that Reilly himself was eager to get to grips with the Bolsheviks.

Although Reilly was inclined to the left in his politics, he seemed to have a personal hatred for the Red leaders. To him they were but a collection of alien and cowardly riff-raff. His perverse anti-Semitism emerged again. He considered it was the Social-Revolutionaries who had really fought for a new régime. Now they had been ousted by a gang of Poles, Georgians and Armenians and a horde of Jews who for most of the time had waited in safety outside Russia until the real revolutionaries had done their work. And it was indeed true that in 1918, of all the commissars on the Soviet Central Executive Committee, only six, including Lenin himself, were wholly Russian.

At the end of April 1918, armed with a pass from Litvinoff, the representative of the Bolsheviks in London, to whom Lloyd George had recommended him, Reilly set out for Russia on the biggest assignment of his career.

His arrival in Russia was not altogether auspicious. On reaching Murmansk, Reilly was promptly arrested by the Royal Navy, who were in charge of British interests in the port, and placed in the lock-up of H.M.S. *Glory*. On the pass made out by Litvinoff his name had been mis-spelt as Reilli; further, its bearer did not appear to be as Irish as he maintained. Admiral Kemp,* Officer Commanding White Sea, sent for Major Stephen Alley, M.C. Major Alley, who had been born and brought up in Russia, had been chief of the British Secret Service in Russia until April, 1918 and was then on his way out of the country, having been recalled to London. He interviewed Reilly in a cell aboard H.M.S. *Glory*, where Reilly produced a message for Bruce Lockhart on a microscopic piece of paper. He had hidden the message, which was in an M.I.1C. code, under the cork of an aspirin bottle. Reilly was released and proceeded with haste to Petrograd. Later he and Alley were to become firm friends.

It was a very different Petrograd to which the now forty-four-year-old Reilly returned. The statue of

* Rear-Admiral T. W. Kemp, C.B., C.M.G., C.I.E.

Alexander III stood, as before, outside the Nicolai station. The waters of the River Neva were as still as when he last saw them, the fortress of Peter and Paul loomed large as ever against the satin blue sky, but the Nevsky Prospect* was largely deserted, unswept for weeks. Dead horses, victims of starvation, lay on the streets.

Reilly was eager to reach Moscow as soon as possible and only stayed long enough in Petrograd to make contact with Commander Ernest Boyce, the new head of the British S.I.S. in Russia since the departure of Major Alley. Boyce was mainly concerned with intelligence operations against Germany and Reilly's was an entirely independent assignment. Reilly made arrangements to use Boyce's cipher staff in the British Consulate-General in Moscow.

Reilly arrived in Moscow on May 7th. It was already summer, when the dust from the narrow, badly built streets could be nauseating, but to Reilly the air of the new Russian capital was invigorating. The Moscow of 1918 was beautiful only in the half-light of early dawn when the absence of humanity gave an illusion of breadth and an artificial splendour to its dingy streets despite the poverty of the surrounding red brick buildings. When Reilly set foot in Moscow it was not early dawn but dusk, yet the streets seemed alive and inviting. He missed only the ragged barefoot band of urchins who had sold roses in pre-Revolution days. He was exhilarated by his sense of mission.

Everything Reilly did was invariably done in the grand manner. If it was Bolsheviks with whom he had to deal, then he would start at the top. Although it was

* The main thoroughfare of Petrograd.

late in the evening when he reached Moscow, Reilly went straight to the Kremlin. Banging on the great red gates, he demanded of the astonished sentries to see Lenin at once. It is unfortunate that Lenin was not available – the two were destined never to meet – as it would have been interesting to have known Lenin's opinion of the man who planned to topple him from power. Reilly, however, did succeed in seeing Bonch-Brouevich, Lenin's closest personal friend. He told him he had been specially sent out by Lloyd George to obtain first-hand information about Bolshevik aims. The British Government was not satisfied, he said, with the reports it received from Bruce Lock-hart.

The sheer audacity of Reilly's plan to penetrate, on his very first day in Moscow, the inner ring of the Kremlin hierarchy was almost incredible. But Kara-chan, one of the Soviet commissars for Foreign Affairs, was suspicious and went straight to Bruce Lockhart. Fortunately the latter was able to allay his suspicions and Reilly went underground to adopt other and more devious tactics.

Disguised as Mr. Constantine, a Greek from the Levant, Reilly returned to Petrograd and sought out his old friend Sasha Grammatikoff who was living in comparative safety, thanks to his friendship with Vladimir Orloff, a Tsarist who under the name of Orlinsky had infiltrated into the Cheka* and had become a senior official at the Cheka's headquarters in Petrograd. Orloff provided Reilly with a pass in the name of Constantine which, with the Cheka stamp on

* Chresvychainaya Kumissaya or 'Extra-ordinary Commission' for Combating Counter-Revolution, Sabotage and Speculation, the successor of the Ochrana and forerunner of the G.P.U. and N.K.V.D.

it, enabled Reilly to move about with little danger of serious interrogation. In Petrograd itself, Reilly established a local headquarters for himself under yet another identity – that of Mr. Massino, a Turkish merchant from the Far East. This was at 10, Torgovaya Ulitza, the home of one of Reilly's old flames, Elena Mikailovna. Again he succeeded in acquiring identity papers in the name of Massino from Orloff, although it is not clear why he should have chosen the name Massino which was Nadine's surname.

For some time, Reilly lived in Petrograd as Mr. Massino and in Moscow as Mr. Constantine. Travelling south to Moscow, he used the identity papers of Mr. Massino, but on arrival in Moscow, Massino would 'disappear'. When journeying from Moscow to Petrograd, he would show the papers of Mr. Constantine who would similarly 'disappear' on arrival in the former capital.

Everywhere were the grim gaunt men in the long grey coats with enormous Mauser pistols strapped to their shoulders – the dreaded figures of Dzerjinsky's* Cheka. Many could neither read nor write and could only just recognize an official Cheka stamp on identity papers. To travel even legitimately was a risk; any suspicious behaviour would result in arrest.

In Moscow, Reilly set up his main headquarters in the Cheremetoff Pereulok in the flat of Grammatikoff's niece, Dagmara.

Dagmara, a dancer at the Moscow Arts Theatre, shared the flat with two other young actresses and it was not long before Reilly's sexual magnetism began to have its effect on this female trio. Soon there was

* The head of the Cheka.

little they would not do for Reilly and his cause. During his assignment in Russia, Reilly amassed a number of mistresses whose help to him was invaluable, but it was in the bed of Dagmara that he was the most often to be found.

In Moscow, Reilly held secret meetings with most of the leading counter-revolutionaries. He was surprised at the widespread anti-Bolshevik feeling even among the working classes. This gave him complete confidence that he would not fail in his mission. If his great hero, the obscure junior officer from Corsica, could conquer France and most of Europe, he saw no reason why he himself should not capture Moscow. As Bruce Lockhart later said of him, he was a man cast in the Napoleonic mould.

Before Reilly moved against Lenin, he had to have an alternative government ready. As the future head of the Russian army, he picked the ex-Tsarist General Yudenich, who claimed that there were thousands of Tsarist officers in and around Moscow who would mobilise at his command. To Grammatikoff, Reilly assigned the role of Minister of Interior, while another old business friend, Chubersky, was given the important post of Minister of Communications. It was vital that telephones, railways and roads should be taken immediately from Bolshevik control and contact established as soon as possible with counter-revolutionary movements elsewhere in Russia. Once Yudenich had captured Moscow, he would join up with the Social-Revolutionary army fighting against Bolshevik troops some distance from Moscow. Later, contact would be made with the White Russian generals in the South who were also holding out against the Reds. Reilly himself would direct the whole counter-revolution.

Once success was assured, a provisional government would take over pending elections.

Reilly spent most of June and July making administrative plans for his new Government and setting up counter-revolutionary 'cells' in both Moscow and Petrograd. For his personal use he organized several more hide-outs in both cities.

Periodically, he handed in reports to one of Boyce's men in Moscow who would cipher them for London in the British Consulate-General then located in Prince Yussopoff's old palace. In Petrograd he occasionally saw Boyce and also Captain Cromie, R.N., the British naval attaché, who had remained in Petrograd after the bulk of the Embassy staff had been evacuated to England in January. Cromie was determined that the Russian fleet should not fall into German hands. Only rarely did Reilly make contact with Bruce Lockhart at his Moscow headquarters in the Elite Hotel; it was important not to compromise the leader of the British Mission.

As anti-Bolshevik activity grew, Red agents-provocateurs appeared in increasing numbers. Reilly had one solution only when these were unmasked – a bullet through the head. Everywhere the Cheka were arresting and interrogating people at random and travelling for Reilly became highly dangerous. But not for long; he neatly solved the problem by obtaining from Grammatikoff's friend, Orloff, identity papers for a member of the Cheka itself. As Comrade Relinsky, plain-clothes agent of the Cheka, he could move with complete freedom. He could threaten with punishment any uniformed Cheka police who delayed him with questions.

None the less, Reilly had his moments of danger.

Once Chekists trapped him in a girl friend's flat. Naked except for his socks, he disappeared from the flat as if by magic to the mystification of his mistress and the Cheka who found Reilly's suit, shirt, underwear and shoes – but not Reilly! He was bold enough to re-appear at the flat an hour later quite unruffled and dressed in another suit, but he refused to explain how he had managed to vanish.

On another occasion, when he was going by train to Petrograd, the Cheka stopped the train to search for him. But Reilly, in Russian sailor's uniform, was as busy as everyone else on the train hunting for the British spy. Anticipating such a search, he had quietly knocked out a sailor in the lavatory compartment, stripped him of his uniform and tipped the man out of the window.

Reilly soon found that he was not the only Allied agent working against the Bolsheviks. The French Secret Service headed by Colonel de Vertement, a small, dapper man, was creating unrest in Siberia, where the Russians held many Czech prisoners of war. Co-operation between the Allies was sadly lacking: while Bruce Lockhart was negotiating with Trotsky for the evacuation of the Czechs to the west so that they could fight against the Germans, de Vertement was trying to persuade the Czechs to take up arms under French officers against the Russians. The French Secret Service headquarters was piled high with bombs and dynamite for sabotage operations. When the Czech revolt in Siberia took place under the twenty-six-year-old General Cajda, anti-Bolshevik resistance increased everywhere.

On July 6th, the German Ambassador, Count von Mirbach, was assassinated by Blumkin, a Social-

Revolutionary who, by coincidence, lived in the room next to Bruce Lockhart's in his hotel. The hope of the counter-revolutionaries was that von Mirbach's murder would provoke Germany into re-opening hostilities against Russia, that the Bolsheviks would consequently fall and that Russia would once again fight alongside her former allies.

On the same day, an all-Russian Congress of 800 delegates, including some of what was still the 'official opposition' of Left Social-Revolutionaries, was gathered in the Moscow Opera House. One of their leaders was the young Maria Spiridonova, who had assassinated one of the Tsar's cruellest governors and was subsequently raped many times over by Cossacks. On the first day of the Congress she had made a violent attack on Lenin in which she accused him of betraying the peasants for his own ends and of 'treating them like dung'. Mirbach's murder was also the signal for a rising of the Left Social-Revolutionaries in Moscow. But at the Moscow Opera House, the top Bolshevik leaders were that day conspicuous by their absence: they had been forewarned by Cheka agents-provocateurs. The explosion of a hand grenade in the Opera House caused pandemonium but killed only the sentry who dropped it.

Some of the counter-revolutionaries had moved too soon and although they had succeeded in arresting and holding for a short time no less a person than Dzerjinsky himself, the *coup d'état* was attempted before Reilly was ready. When he learnt from his ubiquitous spies that the Bolsheviks were prepared for the attempted coup, he raced to the Opera House to warn Bruce Lockhart, some French secret agents and some of his own agents that the theatre was being surrounded by troops and that all exits were barred. On reaching Bruce Lockhart's box in the theatre, afraid that he might himself be arrested, Reilly destroyed all compromising documents, tearing them into tiny fragments and swallowing them or tucking them down the sides of the chairs. On the big stage, where the great Chaliapin had sung *Boris Godunoff* and had later been forced to sing *The Red Flag* to the Communists, there was turmoil.

The counter-revolution which had been led by Alexandrovich* quickly petered out. Alexandrovich was shot and Spiridonova was thrown into the Kremlin. Dzerjinsky, the fanatical Pole, whose piercing eyes it was said had never been seen to blink, began to wreak vengeance.

The apostle of terror, Dzerjinsky, was not only a fanatic who had even put to death his own mother, but was also the greatest organizer among the Bolsheviks after Lenin. He was responsible for indescribable tortures to thousands of innocent people and once said that if he thought it would further the cause of Communism he would order the murder of every bourgeois child in the world. If Lenin was the intellect behind the revolution, Dzerjinsky was the fire. The Red Terror had begun. In the next few days thousands were taken by day or hauled from their beds at night to face the cold ferocity of the Cheka firing squads. Ten days later, on July 16th, the Tsar and his family were slaughtered and their bodies thrown down the shaft of a coal mine. With grim relentless determination Lenin had made it clear that the 300-year-old rule of the Romanoffs was definitely over.

* Alexandrovich was one of the leaders of the Left Social-Revolutionaries.

As Bruce Lockhart later reported to the Foreign Office: 'The Bolsheviks have established a rule of force and oppression unequalled in the history of autocracy. Thousands of men and women have been executed without even the mockery of a trial and thousands more are left to rot in the prisons under conditions to find a parallel to which one must turn to the darkest annals of Indian and Chinese history.'

Reilly, whose Cheka pass had admitted him into and out of the Moscow Opera House, went underground once again to regroup his forces. Although his colleagues and Bruce Lockhart had not been arrested, Trotsky issued an order that all Allied officers were forbidden to travel and Bruce Lockhart was warned that he might have to be placed under 'protective' guard.

Reilly conferred with de Vertement, the head of the French Secret Service in Russia, and pressed him to increase his supply of funds to Boris Savinkoff and his 'League for the Regeneration and Freedom of Russia' whom the French were already financing and who, with several thousand troops had seized Yaroslavl,* a few hundred miles north of Moscow. Reilly used his own funds mainly to support his own agents and the counter-revolutionary organizations in Moscow and Petrograd.

Reilly obtained his funds partly from Bruce Lockhart in Moscow, partly through donations from the Russian bourgeoisie and partly through black market operations.

---

* Savinkoff's attack on Yaroslavl was intended to coincide with the Allied landings at Archangel. These, unknown to Savinkoff, were postponed a fortnight. After valiant fighting by the anti-Bolsheviks, the Reds eventually recaptured the town. Savinkoff was very bitter at the Allied delay.

Many of the aristocracy and bourgeoisie still had plenty of money and, as the Bolsheviks had not yet closed all the cabarets, were still crowding into Yards, a *café-chantant* in the Petrovsky Park, and Jan's, a night-club which only opened at five a.m. to serve champagne breakfasts. But the rich had neither food nor fuel; Reilly supplied both.

In addition to seeking French cooperation, Reilly also maintained close links with the U.S. Secret Service which, under Kalamatiano, an American of Greek extraction, was also conducting its own anti-Red operations.

Reilly's energy was astounding. In the heat of the Moscow summer, throughout the day and often all through the night as well, he went the rounds of his agents and spies in the search for possible collaborators among people in high places. Since the failure of the Alexandrovich coup, he had had to reorganize his whole movement, and weed out the weak links and suspected agents-provocateurs. Constantly on the move, going from one agent's hide-out to another, from café to café for pre-arranged meetings, travelling to and from Petrograd, Comrade Relinsky seemed to be everywhere at once.

By mid-July, it was clear that a landing of Allied troops in North Russia was imminent. On July 23rd, the Allied Embassies in Vologda left for Archangel. Bruce Lockhart was isolated in Moscow; although personally he disagreed with the policy of intervention, when he realized his views were not shared in London and that intervention was inevitable, he decided to comply with the War Cabinet policy. From the beginning of June, on orders from the British Government, he had worked actively for intervention, a movement directed not against Germany but against the *de facto* Government of Russia. As he said, 'I did my best to ensure that intervention would have at least some chance of success.'

On August 4th, the Allies landed at Archangel, but in pitiful numbers – a move doomed to failure from the start. Soviet reaction was quick. Bruce Lockhart's headquarters were requisitioned by the Bolsheviks, the Cheka raided the British Consulate-General where Boyce's clerical staff who sent Reilly's reports to London only just managed to burn their ciphers in time.

By now Reilly was nearly ready to act but he was frustrated by the lack of funds of the various counter-revolutionary and pro-Allied organizations. Bruce Lockhart came to his aid. In exchange for promissory notes, payable in pounds sterling in London, he collected a mass of roubles from Russians who were delighted at the opportunity to receive sterling in exchange. A total of 8,400,000 roubles* was collected for Bruce Lockhart by the small British firm of W. B. Combes Higgs alone. Reilly kept what amounted to his own private bank at Dagmara's flat and from here he and his agents would distribute hundreds of thousands of roubles to the anti-Bolsheviks. Funds provided by Bruce Lockhart also went to Savinkoff and to General Alexeiev who, with a small army of ex-Tsarist officers and Cossacks, was fighting Red forces south of the Don.

Reilly was now also in constant touch with another British agent, 'I.K.8'. This was Captain George Hill,† who was head of a separate intelligence organization responsible to the Director of Military Intelligence at

---

* About £240,000 at the exchange rate of the time.
† Later Brigadier G. A. Hill, D.S.O., O.B.E., M.C.

the War Office. Hill was an outstandingly brave man and one of the first ever to land by plane behind the enemy lines. He had operated a team of spies who were landed by plane behind the enemy front in Bulgaria. He had had a hair-raising experience transporting the Rumanian crown jewels through five battle-fronts from Moscow to Jassy, the new Rumanian capital. In Moscow, his prime task was to collect intelligence about German troop movements, but in order to keep himself informed on Russian plans, he had managed to become Trotsky's Air Adviser and had helped him organize his own Intelligence Service. Continually harassed by Colonel Rudolf Bauer, head of the German Secret Service in Russia, Hill had been organizing bands of guerrillas, which consisted mainly of ex-Tsarist officers, to harry the German army. He had developed his own widespread communications system which consisted of a small band of Lett and Estonian couriers who carried his messages to and from Moscow through all four points of the compass. Soon after the Allied landing at Archangel, the Russians issued an order for Hill's arrest, but with no less than eight secret head-quarters ready for such an event Hill changed his name to Bergmann and went underground.

First, however, he conferred with Bruce Lockhart and Reilly. They agreed that although Hill was to go underground he would continue to operate independently from Reilly. It was arranged, nevertheless, that they would keep each other informed of their activities and meet each day at fixed times in the Tverskoy Park.

Even before the British in Moscow were forced to burn their ciphers, communications by telegraph or telephone in and out of Moscow were repeatedly being cut. Reilly, Bruce Lockhart and Hill were now reduced to using a small pocket-dictionary code,* and Hill's Lettish and Estonian couriers proved invaluable to Reilly. Although occasionally the Cheka would seize a courier, most of Reilly's coded messages, which were typed on linen and sewn in to the collars of the couriers' jackets, reached their destinations. Bruce Lockhart used Swedish couriers attached to the Swedish Consulate.

It was about this time that Boyce, who was himself travelling frequently between Petrograd and Moscow, disposed of what became notorious as the 'Sissons Documents'. The various intelligence services operating in Russia paid well for information and Boyce had spent a considerable sum for some correspondence which seemed to prove conclusively that the Bolsheviks were in secret liaison with the German High Command and that the British War Cabinet's belief that Lenin and Trotsky were German agents was correct. When Reilly examined this correspondence with Hill, he discovered that although the letters purported to come from different parts of Russia, they were all typed on the same typewriter. As the whole correspondence was obviously faked, Reilly suggested to Boyce that he should re-sell it to the Americans. Boyce did so. Mr. Sissons of the U.S. mission in Petrograd paid a very large amount for the documents and Boyce made a profit on the deal.

By mid-August, Reilly's one concern was the inefficient organization of his 'troops' in Moscow, Yudenich's ex-Tsarist officers. There was no doubt

---

* Users of the dictionary code had a 'key' which consisted of a scale like a ruler for numbering off the words in each column of the dictionary. Coded, the word 'sabotage', for instance, might be 064-14, meaning the fourteenth word down the column on page sixty-four. The dictionary used was a small Anglo-German pocket edition.

about their bravery, but he was far from satisfied with their discipline and feared they would be incapable of working to the very strict timetable he had worked out. Reilly's grand plan was to arrest all the Red leaders in one swoop on August 28th when a meeting of the Soviet Central Executive Committee was due to be held. Rather than execute them, Reilly intended to de-bag the Bolshevik hierarchy and, with Lenin and Trotsky in front, to march them through the streets of Moscow bereft of trousers and underpants, shirt-tails flying in the breeze. They would then be imprisoned. Reilly maintained that it was better to destroy their power by ridicule than to make martyrs of the Bolshevik leaders by shooting them.

Meanwhile funds were still being distributed to the counter-revolutionaries. Nor was the Russian Orthodox Church forgotten. Marxism was the religion of anti-Christ and to ensure the support of the Church, one day in August, Reilly and Hill called on Archbishop Tikhon, Grand Metropolitan of Moscow and Patriarch of the Russian Church with two large suitcases containing five million roubles* which Bruce Lockhart had supplied. It was probably the largest cash donation ever to be placed in an offertory box. Two years later, another great British spy, Paul Dukes,† was to report from Russia: 'There is only one man in the whole of Russia whom the Bolsheviks fear from the bottom of their hearts, and that is Tikhon, the Patriarch of the Russian Church.'

The Red Army in 1918 was a rabble and quite unreliable. For their *élite* troops, the Bolshevik leaders relied on the mercenary regiments of Letts. (Latvia

* About £143,000 at the exchange rate of the time.
† Later Sir Paul Dukes, K.B.E.

itself had been overrun by the Germans). Soon after the Allies had landed at Archangel, Colonel Berzin, in command of one of the three Lettish regiments, together with another Lett called Schmidhen, who had a letter of recommendation from Captain Cromie, called on Bruce Lockhart. The Letts, they said, had no wish to fight for the Bolsheviks against the Allies. They asked Bruce Lockhart to put them in touch with the Allied forces in Archangel. Bruce Lockhart gave the two men passes to Archangel and put them in touch with Reilly.

To Reilly, Berzin's arrival was very opportune. It was a Lettish regiment which was to guard the theatre where the Soviet Central Executive Committee was to meet. What could be more appropriate than to arrest Lenin and Trotsky with their own guards? The Letts despised the Russians and within forty-eight hours, as a result of several meetings between Reilly and Berzin in the Tramble Café in the Tverskoy Boulevard, all plans were made. The chests of drawers in Dagmara's flat were nearly emptied of roubles to ensure the loyalty of Berzin and his fellow officers. Reilly promised them much more when the coup had succeeded. Moscow waited its hour.

Although the meeting of the Bolshevik leaders was postponed to September 6th, this did not worry Reilly. It gave him time to go to Petrograd to see Captain Cromie – since Boyce was now in Moscow – and perfect his plans for an uprising in the former Russian capital to coincide with his coup in Moscow. Before leaving for Petrograd he confided his plans to de Vertement and the French Secret Service.

From then on events moved with unexpected speed. The day after Reilly left Moscow, and unknown to him until a few days later, the Cheka swooped on the French Secret Service headquarters in Moscow. De Vertement made a dramatic escape over the rooftops but Dzerjinsky's men found a quantity of explosives and captured six French agents who were accused of taking part with Lettish agents in an Allied plot to overthrow the Soviet Government. When Hill learnt the news, he immediately sent a courier to Petrograd to warn Reilly but the messenger never reached his destination. He too was arrested by the Cheka but was fortunately not suspected of his connections with Reilly and Hill. The following day, Reilly finalized his plans in Petrograd but he was alarmed to find that two of his hide-outs in the city had been raided. Evidently the Cheka were after him and, on the eve of the achievement of his ambitions, he felt the bitter taste of doubt and a crushing anticipation of calamity. On the same day, worried by a sudden increase in the number of their men who were being arrested, the counter-revolutionaries became trigger-happy. Uritsky, head of the Petrograd Cheka and a merciless butcher himself, was assassinated.

On the next day, August 31st, Dora Kaplan, a Social-Revolutionary, fired two bullets at point-blank range at Lenin as he was leaving a meeting in Moscow. It was a miracle he was not killed outright and his chances of living were considered slight. During the night, Bruce Lockhart was arrested at gun-point and taken to Cheka headquarters in the Loubianka. There he was placed in a room in the 'Kennels'* with Dora Kaplan and

* 'The Kennels' was the name given to the temporary accommodations for prisoners in Cheka headquarters. After initial interrogation, prisoners were usually placed either in the 'Inner Prison' at the Cheka H.Q. or in the Butyrsky Martial Investigation Prison.

interrogated by Peters, Vice-President of the Cheka and Dzerjinsky's chief assistant. Peters, wearing a leather jacket and khaki trousers and carrying a huge Mauser, wanted to know what his relationship was with Lenin's would-be assassin and where Reilly was. Bruce Lockhart insisted on his diplomatic privileges and refused to answer. He destroyed a compromising notebook in the Cheka lavatories in full view of two armed guards. The Cheka did not run to toilet paper and the use of the notebook pages instead aroused no suspicion. Bruce Lockhart was released but his freedom was to be only temporary. While he was in the Loubianka, his flat had been ransacked.

As for Dora Kaplan she was shot by Malkoff, Commandant of the Kremlin, personally, without knowing whether her attempt on Lenin's life had been successful. It was said that she went to her death in a state of exaltation.

On the same day that Bruce Lockhart was arrested, Reilly, who was still in Petrograd, realized that his plans had gone wrong. Unshaven and disguised as a workman, he tried to make contact with Captain Cromie in his office at the former British Embassy. He was too late; Cheka gunmen, searching for Reilly, had raided the premises. The gallant Cromie had resisted to the last; with a Browning in each hand he had killed a commissar and wounded several Cheka thugs, before falling himself riddled with Red bullets. Kicked and trampled on, his body was thrown out of a second floor window.

Permission for an English chaplain to say prayers over the body was refused but the next day the Netherlands Minister in Russia, who was looking after British interests in Petrograd, succeeded in recovering the body and in arranging a funeral. The Swiss Minister was also at the graveside to express 'my deep sympathy and admiration for the late Captain Cromie who has died for his country'.

In revenge for the attempt on Lenin, Dzerjinsky's firing squads went into action again; 500 people were shot in Moscow and a further 700 in Petrograd. Elsewhere in Russia, over 8,000 were said to have been executed in a systematic annihilation of Bolshevism's possible enemies. In Moscow no prominent Social-Revolutionary remained except those who lay on or in the ground with bullets through their heads.

The Bolshevik press howled for blood and still more blood: 'We will make our hearts cruel, hard and immovable so that no mercy will enter them. Without mercy, without sparing, we will kill our enemies in scores of hundreds; let them drown themselves in their own blood. Let there be floods of blood of the bourgeois – more blood, as much as possible.' The Council of the People's Commissaries declared: 'It is necessary to safeguard our position by means of Terror.' The Petrograd Soviet asked that enemies of the proletariat be executed 'not only by hundreds, as is the case now, but by thousands'. Zinoviev, one of Lenin's closest friends, called for the annihilation of ten million anti-Bolsheviks.

Reilly was now thoroughly concerned and decided to return to Moscow at once. His Cheka pass got him safely aboard the train from Petrograd but even with a pass he dared not face the inspection at the station barriers at Moscow. He left the train at Kline, a station forty miles outside Moscow, and made a series of hitch-hike trips by horse and cart along a primitive road to the capital.

The Moscow papers were full of what they called the 'Lockhart Plot'. In banner headlines, the Russian press denounced the 'Anglo-French bandits' who had plotted to murder both Lenin and Trotsky and overthrow the Soviet Government. Bruce Lockhart was named as the arch-criminal and Reilly as his chief spy; the Lettish Colonel Berzin was said to have confessed. *Pravda* demanded that the 'scoundrels' be handed over to the Revolutionary Tribunal and shot. There were photographs and descriptions of Reilly not only in the press but on placards throughout the city which announced a 100,000 rouble reward for Reilly's capture – dead or alive. The Cheka were instructed to shoot him on sight.

The Cheka arrested no less than eight women who, on interrogation, admitted to being Reilly's wife. They were all placed in the same cell along with some thirty other women. Reilly's wives came from all walks of life and ranged from an actress to the daughter of a concierge; they had two things in common – all were young and beautiful. It is not known whether Reilly went through a form of marriage with all of them – a simple matter in the Russia of 1918 – but a friend of Bruce Lockhart and Hill, who was in the same prison, said that the furious jealousy and fighting between the eight wives had to be seen to be believed. The ultimate fate of these women is uncertain.

With his plans in ruins round his neck Reilly dared not visit any of his former hide-outs. Instead, he made his way to the Malaia Bronnaia, a nest of cheap garrets off the Tverskoy Boulevard, to the apartment of a White Russian whose loyalty was unquestioned but with whom he himself had never previously made contact. He was not actively concerned in Reilly's counter-revolution plans and was probably not under Cheka suspicion. From here he managed to get a message to Dagmara, who fortunately had not been arrested.

From Dagmara he learnt of the repelling violence of the Cheka reprisals. He heard that Bruce Lockhart had been re-arrested and imprisoned once again in the Loubianka, but that Hill was fortunately underground and safe. Disguised with a beard and under the name of Bergmann, Hill was working by night developing news-reel films for the Russian cinemas. By day he was still keeping his courier service going. So far as Hill knew his organization was uncompromised.

There had, however, been tragedy at Dagmara's flat the previous day when the Cheka had made a routine search of the flat, not specifically in search of Reilly. Fortunately Dagmara had been able to conceal in her knickers the mass of rouble notes which Reilly kept in the flat. Under her voluminous dress nothing could be seen. While the Cheka were going through her flat, one of Hill's messengers had arrived.

Hill, realizing that Reilly's position had become untenable, if indeed he had not been arrested, had sent one of his best messengers, a girl called Vi, to tell Dagmara that he was ready to take over Reilly's organization. On seeing the Chekists, Vi was clever enough not to reveal her agitation, stating she was merely a seamstress delivering a new blouse. (In Moscow, Hill made a practice of using female messengers who always carried carefully packed handmade blouses for just such an emergency.) Soon after the departure of Vi, however, a girl messenger of the U.S. Secret Service arrived at the flat with messages for Reilly. At the sight of the Cheka, she had gone into hysterics and although Dagmara had persuaded the Cheka of her own innocence, both Dagmara's actress friends and the

American messenger were arrested. Kalamatiano himself had, as a result, been arrested that afternoon. Later he was shot.

Reilly listened to this grave news without showing any emotion and immediately despatched Dagmara to tell Hill he was safe and to ask Hill to come round straight away.

Hill found Reilly calm and unperturbed, and anxious only to regroup his forces once again and renew the fight as soon as possible. As an alternative, Reilly discussed the advisability of giving himself up to the Cheka in the hope that the Russians would then release Bruce Lockhart who was now in solitary confinement in the Kremlin. Wisely, Hill advised against this: the Russians would merely hold Reilly as well as Bruce Lockhart and both would probably be shot. He urged Reilly, in the interests of the Secret Service, to escape from Russia as soon as possible and make for London to report in person all that had happened.

Reilly and Hill discussed at length the question of who had given the plot away. Reilly was convinced that the betrayal of his plans could not have come from anyone within his own organization. Apart from the leaders of the planned coup and the commandants of the Lettish regiments, no-one had known the full details. If Berzin had confessed, it could only have been because he himself had been betrayed and tortured. Reilly considered the French; de Vertement and his colleagues he could trust but he remembered their constant association with a French journalist called René Marchand, Moscow correspondent of the Paris newspaper *Figaro*. Reilly had never trusted Marchand and wondered whether he could have been the traitor.

Reilly decided to take Hill's advice and make for London. While Hill made preparations for his departure, Reilly spent three days in hiding, in a different place each day. He slept with his clothes and boots on. When he had run out of hide-outs with reliable contacts, he was forced to spend a fourth day in the room of a prostitute who was in the last stages of syphilis and whose apartment reeked of mahorca, the cheap tobacco smoked by soldiers and peasants. Each day, at pre-arranged times, he would meet Hill at the Paskeller Café and finally, equipped with Hill's own passport in the name of Bergmann, Reilly set off for Petrograd for the last time.

As a parting gift, Hill gave him his pair of fine tortoiseshell hairbrushes which Reilly had coveted. On one occasion when Reilly and Hill had been walking together in the streets of Moscow, Dzerjinsky had passed in his Rolls-Royce – a car in which the head of the Cheka had once sent Bruce Lockhart on a tour of the city to see for himself the corpses of anarchist bands which the Cheka had mown down. On seeing the car, Hill said to Reilly:

'When your counter-revolution has succeeded, you can make a present to me of Dzerjinsky's Rolls-Royce!'

Reilly had replied:

'Certainly, Hillishka, if you give me your hair-brushes in return.'

On the train to Petrograd, Reilly struck up an acquaintance with a German diplomat and by passing himself off as one of his colleagues, Reilly reached Petrograd in safety, but not without a few scares from continual Cheka inspections of papers on the way.

After spending a fortnight in hiding in Petrograd, Reilly eventually made contact with a Dutch trader who had a ship lying in the river Neva. He paid him 60,000 roubles to be smuggled out of Russia. Reilly expected the boat to go direct to Stockholm, but, to his consternation, it stopped *en route* at the German naval base at Reval. Despite his harrowing experience in Russia, Reilly was unwilling to miss an opportunity to pick up intelligence. Before sailing for Sweden he had the audacity to invite himself to dinner at the naval officers' mess, posing as a Balt who was well disposed towards Germany.

While Reilly was making his way back to England, in Moscow the full story of his betrayal appeared in the Russian press. The traitor had indeed been René Marchand, the French journalist. He admitted this himself and after the war returned to France to join the French Communist Party.

In publishing Marchand's revelations, the Russian press congratulated the traitor as 'being an honest person and indignant at the treachery of the Allied representatives'. Reilly's efforts to free the Russian people from the yoke of Bolshevism were denounced as 'bandit-like methods that had no connection with the struggle against Germany and were intended to throw Russia into a worse crisis and bloody conflict.'

Thus ended Reilly's great dream. But for the stupidity of the French Secret Service in admitting an outsider into their inner councils, the whole course of history might have been changed. Instead, Communism is still with us today and Soviet success in foiling the 'Lockhart Plot' has been recorded for posterity by the Russian playwright Pogodin whose play *Vichi Vrazh-*

*debnye** is performed by the Russian repertory theatre to this day and was the subject of a film produced in 1957.

* *Whirlwinds of Trouble.*

VIII

For freedom's battle once begun.

BYRON

The British had countered the Russian arrests of Bruce
Lockhart and others by arresting Litvinoff, the Bolshevik Government's representative in London, and holding him in Brixton Prison. An exchange of prisoners
had been arranged and while Reilly was secretly finding
his own way back to England, Bruce Lockhart and Hill,
together with Boyce,* who had been arrested and
thrown into a common gaol but released under the
exchange agreement, set off for London on October
2nd. They travelled to the Finnish frontier in a special
train guarded by Lett soldiers. On reaching Finland,
however, Hill received orders from London to return
to Russia for a few weeks to blow up bridges and carry
out other sabotage work. Bruce Lockhart, Boyce and
some other British personnel who accompanied them
continued to Sweden and eventually reached Aberdeen
on October 18th.

* Boyce and other Allied personnel gaoled by the Bolsheviks were
herded with Russian criminals, fifty to sixty to a room; their only
sustenance was a daily helping of cabbage water and a little piece of
black bread. But for the help of the American Red Cross they would
never have survived.

Reilly, who travelled by boat from Reval to Sweden and thence overland to Bergen, arrived back in London early in November and was immediately awarded the Military Cross. A D.S.O. was not considered advisable in case it attracted attention and, for security reasons, even his M.C. was not gazetted until 1920.

On Reilly's arrival in London, such was the lack of inter-departmental liaison in Whitehall that, while Cumming was busy arranging for him to be awarded the M.C., the Foreign Office were doubting his bona fides and Bruce Lockhart had to vouch for his loyalty.

After the months of living in hiding in Moscow and Petrograd with only infrequent opportunities to wash – let alone bathe – Reilly went straight to the Savoy Hotel where he took a suite and entertained Bruce Lockhart and Boyce, over a champagne lunch, with the full story of his escape which he had already told Cumming earlier in the day.

A few days later Hill, who had successfully completed his sabotage mission in Russia, also reached London. Having reported to Colonel Kisch, the Deputy Director of Military Intelligence, Hill was summoned to see Cumming and Lieutenant-Colonel Freddie Browning, his assistant, who, apart from his S.I.S. activities, was also a director of the Savoy Hotel. Hill was delighted to see Reilly in Cumming's office, alive and safe. By this time, Major Alley, who had returned to England a good deal earlier, and Boyce were both established in posts in S.I.S. headquarters in London.

Although Reilly was eager to return to Russia at once to organize another attempt to overthrow the Reds, it was decided that both he and Hill, now transferred from Military Intelligence to the Secret Service proper, should have a period of leave before going to

South Russia in mid-December to obtain inside information on the strength of White Russian resistance under General Denikin.

On November 11th the war with Germany came to an end, and although his personal war against Communism was not over, Reilly celebrated like everyone else. On November 12th, in an immaculate uniform of the Royal Canadian Air Force, he gave a party at the Savoy for Bruce Lockhart, Rex Leeper* and their wives. Later, over supper in his suite, the women were dazzled by Reilly's magnificent claret-coloured silk dressing-gown and much admired his tortoiseshell hairbrushes, quite unaware of how he had received them from Hill.

The following day, Bruce Lockhart took Reilly, Hugh Walpole, who had been doing British propaganda work in Russia in the early part of the war, and Don Gregory† to revive nostalgic memories at the Coliseum where the Russian Ballet was performing. Hill joined them afterwards at another supper party in Reilly's suite at the Savoy. In return for the tortoiseshell brushes he had received from Hill, Reilly gave him a pair of silver hairbrushes inscribed 'From S.T.1'. He apologized for being unable to give him Dzerjinsky's Rolls-Royce!

Reilly's life for the next month was not restricted to

---

* Rex Leeper, now Sir Reginald Leeper, G.B.E., K.C.M.G., was in the Intelligence Department of the Foreign Office. Russia had been his special responsibility, and it was he who had been largely responsible for arranging the exchange of Litvinoff with Bruce Lockhart.
† J. D. Gregory, C.B., C.M.G., then head of the Foreign Office's Northern Department, which included Russia, and later Assistant Under-Secretary of State from 1925–8. Walpole and Gregory were the author's godfathers.

parties with friends and colleagues from Moscow. There were few occasions when there was not a woman in his life and at this time he had an affair with a London prostitute, as he had once many years before. The girl, who was in her early twenties, rejoiced in the extraordinary nickname of 'Plugger'. Fair and very elegantly dressed, she was much attached to the master-spy although she knew nothing of his career.

It was Bruce Lockhart who on his return from Russia received both the credit and the blame for the plot that failed. Reilly's name was not, and indeed for security reasons, could not be mentioned. In October and November, 1918, the question of Bruce Lockhart and his activities was raised on no less than eight different occasions in the House of Commons by Ramsay MacDonald and by Joseph King, the Liberal M.P. for North Somerset.

MacDonald and King pressed the Government for details of the circumstances that led to Bruce Lockhart's arrest and asked for a full report on his work in Russia. Arthur Balfour, the Secretary of State for Foreign Affairs and his Under-Secretary, Lord Robert Cecil, successfully parried all questions and gave nothing away.

This was not good enough for King who, on November 14th, made a violent attack on the Government's whole policy toward Russia and on the misuse of Secret Service funds. These were the highlights of his speech which ran to several columns in Hansard:

I refer to the remarkable case of Mr. Lockhart who returned to his country on 19th October and whose report upon very important event is not yet available . . . Litvinoff's letter to Trotsky about this fellow

Lockhart was to this effect: 'This will introduce to you a gentleman of popular democratic opinions. He is a good fellow, treat him well' . . . After he had been there a little time, Mr. Lockhart proceeded, unfortunately, to receive instructions from England, which were that he was to use Secret Service money with the object of overturning the man to whom he had brought the recommendation. This Mr. Lockhart proceeded to do . . . Mr. Lockhart offered money to this man and that . . . He went to a Lettish officer and offered him a large sum if, with his soldiers, he would place Mr. Trotsky and Mr. Lenin in his power . . . The facts as I state them are known to the Foreign Secretary; he knows them, because I told him; but when I told him, he told me he knew them before!

King accused the Government of withholding the facts because it might damage its electoral chances: 'We may be sure it (Bruce Lockhart's report) is not going to be communicated to this House before the General Election.' In an oblique reference to Reilly, he went on to say:

In recent months we have immensely increased the amount of Secret Service money and there are papers on record which show that one officer alone passed £120,000 in one week in Russia with the purpose of starting a counter-revolution. What are all these operations which our Government do not dare for a moment to disclose to us?

There was no reply from the Government front bench to this speech – not even an evasive one. It would have been difficult to make a satisfactory answer without admitting that the Reilly plot had failed and that military intervention by Allied forces had been absurdly weak. If Reilly had succeeded in capturing Lenin and Trotsky and had marched them through the streets of Moscow in their shirt-tails no doubt Lloyd George and his colleagues would have taken all the credit.

Meanwhile, the Bolshevists staged a trial in Moscow of a number of those engaged on what they called 'The Lockhart Plot'. Two of the principals, Sidney Reilly and Bruce Lockhart, were judged, *in absentia*, and sentenced to death should they ever set foot again in Russia. But the Cheka held prisoner plenty of others who had been involved with Reilly with which to fill the dock and keep their firing squads occupied. These included Kalamatiano, the head of the American Secret Service, Colonel A. V. Friede, a Russian staff officer who had been one of Reilly's most useful agents, Marie Friede, his sister and one of Reilly's mistresses, and Jeanne Morans, headmistress of the French school in Moscow.

Nor was Marie Friede the only one of Reilly's mistresses in the dock. Beside her stood Mlle Strajenska, a typist from the Soviet All-Russia Central Executive Committee and Mlle Otten, one of the young actresses who had shared Dagmara's flat. Although State Prosecutor Krilenko was scathing in his comments on the young women's sexual relationships with the master spy, he seemed satisfied that they had 'only played a passive part, caught in Reilly's web'. Unlike Kalamatiano, Friede and others, they escaped execution.

In mid-December, after a final briefing from Cumming, Reilly and Hill left for South Russia. Crossing the

Channel by night via the Southampton–Le Havre route, they found all the cabins booked. They had nowhere to sleep but, by chance, an old friend of Reilly's was aboard. Hill was astonished to see Paderewsky, the great pianist, who was returning to Poland to become Prime Minister, greet Reilly as a long-lost friend. Paderewsky allowed Reilly and Hill to doss down in his own cabin and there was much reminiscing about Reilly's sister Anna. It was clear too that at sometime in his life Paderewsky had been a friend of Reilly's mother.

After travelling by train from Le Havre to Marseilles, and thence by a series of trips in British destroyers provided for the purpose, the two British agents arrived in South Russia on Christmas Day, 1918. Armed with 'credentials' from the Department of Overseas Trade, Reilly and Hill posed as two British businessmen who had come to investigate the possibilities of opening up trade with the Russians. Their real task was to make an appreciation of the strength of the White Russian movement under the command of General Denikin.

It was on the whole an uneventful assignment, except for one curious and unexplained incident. One day while walking through Odessa, Reilly and Hill passed a house in Alexander III Boulevard; it was number fifteen. At the sight of this house, Reilly went white and fell down in the street obviously suffering an intense emotional crisis. After a few minutes he recovered but refused to discuss what memories this house had evoked.

Reilly and Hill found that the White Russian position at this time was fairly sound from the purely military standpoint, but that administratively all was chaos. After fourteen days in South Russia, Hill returned to

London to make a preliminary report to Cumming while Reilly stayed on for a further fortnight. A complex system of couriers carried his reports back to London via Istanbul, Bucharest, Budapest and Paris.

As soon as Reilly got back to England at the beginning of February, 1919, Cumming had yet another assignment for him and Hill. They were to attend the Paris Peace Conference. There was a feeling in some official quarters that the White Russians should be the sole representatives of Russia at the Peace Conference. Reilly and Hill were to watch for any moves on the part of either the White Russians or the Bolsheviks.

Cumming arranged with Admiral 'Blinker' Hall,* the Director of Naval Intelligence, that Reilly and Hill should pose as 'Russian experts' attached to the British Naval Mission to the Conference. In Paris, they stayed first at the Majestic Hotel with the rest of the British Naval Mission but to avoid revealing the real purpose of their presence in Paris and compromising the whole Mission, they moved out to the Mercedes Hotel near the Place de l'Etoile after a week.

Late one night, two American observers from Moscow arrived in Paris sponsoring an 'offer' from Chicherin, the Soviet Commissar for Foreign Affairs, that the Bolshevik Government should be represented at the conference. One of the Americans was William Bullitt,† who had been sent to Moscow by President Wilson. Next morning, Reilly and Hill discussed this new move over breakfast with Walford Selby‡ and Harold Nicholson of the Foreign Office. They were

---

* Rear Admiral Sir Reginald Hall, K.C.M.G., C.B.
† The first U.S. Ambassador to the U.S.S.R. from 1933–6.
‡ Later Sir Walford Selby, K.C.M.G., C.B., C.V.O., British Ambassador in Lisbon.

worried that the 'offer' might be favourably received in other quarters besides the U.S.A. The two 'advisers to the Naval Delegation' succeeded in postponing further serious discussion of the subject for twenty-four hours during which time Hill reported the latest development to Wickham Steed, Editor of *The Times*. Steed in turn told Lord Northcliffe and the following day *The Times* and the *Daily Mail* came out with leading articles which ridiculed the two Americans and blew the Bolshevik proposals sky high.

It was at the Majestic Hotel that Reilly first met Winston Churchill and from that moment on he idolized the British statesman. In turn, Reilly introduced Churchill* to Savinkoff, who had escaped from Russia to continue the fight against Bolshevism from the West. If Churchill did not actually idolize Savinkoff, he certainly had a great admiration for him. In the years that followed, Churchill was to give considerable encouragement to Savinkoff and Reilly in their anti-Bolshevik activities.

It was also during the Peace Conference that Reilly first met Major W. Field-Robinson who was in charge of the British S.I.S. Paris office in the Rue Joubert. A great friendship grew up between Reilly and Field-Robinson, or 'Robbie' as he was called, which was to stand both men in good stead in times of crises. Another of 'C's' agents with whom Reilly made friends in Paris was the singer Eleanor Toye. Singing as she did in most of the capitals of Europe, she was a useful member of Cumming's network. Reilly much enjoyed discussing philosophy with her and on one occasion

* Reilly was introduced to Churchill by Sir William Bull, M.P., P.C. Bull was Chairman of London Unionist M.P.s from 1910 to 1929 and a friend of Cumming's.

on the balcony of his hotel spent the whole night expounding to her his ideas about life. By the time he had finished, Paris had started another day's work. Eleanor Toye considered him unscrupuluous in political matters, but a man of absolute integrity in his personal relationships and generous to a fault.

On the completion of their Paris Peace Conference assignment, Hill and Reilly separated. Hill returned to South Russia to co-ordinate the activities of the White Russians in the Caucasus in their struggle against the Reds. Reilly had other business to attend to.

From Paris, Reilly went to New York for a few weeks' leave to see his beloved Nadine. It was two and a half years since husband and wife had met. War changes both history and people and in the case of Nadine, the change had been for the worse. She had not been faithful to Reilly and the reunion was not a success.

While Reilly was in New York, a further complication arose in London. Margaret, who had spent most of the war in Brussels, arrived in England to reclaim her husband. She went to the Foreign Office and demanded to know where her husband was. When he heard of this, Cumming, who knew little more than anyone else about his top spy's private life summoned Hill, who had not yet left for the Caucasus, and instructed him to find out how many wives Reilly really had.

Hill, whose investigations proved inconclusive, decided to tackle Reilly himself about the matter but, on his return from New York, Reilly was totally unforthcoming: 'I have no wife,' he said. 'There is nothing to discuss.' Enraged by what he considered to be impertinent enquiries, Reilly went straight to Cumming. What passed between the two men when they met is not known, but immediately after the meeting Hill was ordered by Cumming to abandon his investigations. Just as quickly, Margaret left London and went back to Brussels. Later, she admitted that she had left England partly because Reilly had paid her £10,000 to do so but mainly because of his threats of what he would do to her if she did not disappear or if she ever mentioned their marriage to anyone.

Cumming was uncertain to what use he could next put Reilly. He kept him loosely on a string in London and Paris while waiting for Government policy and the situation in Russia to clear. The confusion in Whitehall about the attitude Britain should adopt towards the Bolsheviks was almost as great as the confusion among the ranks of the anti-Red refugees escaping from Russia. The British Government hoped for a counter-revolution that would overthrow the Bolsheviks but the Russian aristocracy, bourgeoisie and Social-Revolutionaries who had left Russia were not only unorganized and without funds but at odds with each other.

Because of his many contacts with anti-Bolsheviks of all political persuasions, who were now escaping from Russia to Britain and France in increasing numbers, Reilly was of vital assistance to Cumming in assessing the reliability of the information which the refugees brought out of Russia. Whenever Russia was under discussion in 'C's' headquarters, Reilly was to be found at his chief's elbow. When that master of disguises, Paul Dukes, returned in 1919 from his epic spying exploits in Russia, it was Reilly who greeted him on the platform at King's Cross and whenever Dukes, who had much to report, visited Cumming at S.I.S. headquarters in Whitehall Court, Reilly was always there, 'a sinister man crouching like a panther in the corner of "C's" office'. Here in an ordinary block of flats, in which the Secret Intelligence Service occupied the top three floors and where the commissionaires were Special Branch police in disguise, Reilly, Dukes and Cumming would discuss revolution and counter-revolution. In a downstairs flat ignorant of what went on above his head, lived Bernard Shaw.

Reilly had taken rooms in the Albany, Piccadilly, where he surrounded himself with his Napoleana and lined his walls with expensive books which he ordered by the hundred from Hatchards, just across Piccadilly from his rooms. He engaged a personal valet called Alex Humphreys, whom Reilly's associates described as being as sinister as Reilly himself, and ordered new suits by the dozen from J. Daniels & Co., the leading West End tailors at the corner of Pall Mall and St. James's Street. In the Albany he entertained old friends and new, Dukes, Bruce Lockhart, Boyce, Hill, Alley and many a mysterious Russian. New friends included Sir Archibald Sinclair,* Personal Military Secretary to Winston Churchill,† who was to succeed Lloyd George as Leader of the Liberal Party, Admiral 'Blinker' Hall, the Director of Naval Intelligence, and Sir Basil Thompson, Commissioner of Police and Head of the Special Branch, who had the task of deciding which Russian refugees should be accepted into the country and which suspected Bolsheviks should be deported.

Reilly was an excellent host and a witty conversationalist. He spoke with authority not only on Russia

---

* Later Viscount Thurso.
† Secretary of State for War at the time.

and Russians, but also on many other subjects of which his favourites were history, art, business and religion. Since his marriage to Nadine, he had abandoned Buddhism in favour of the Greek-Orthodox Church but he could talk with authority on almost every religion. If Jesus Christ was Reilly's greatest 'hero', Napoleon and Churchill ranked not far behind. Most of his conversation, however, concerned Russia and his hatred of the Bolsheviks.

Besides entertaining in his rooms at the Albany, Reilly took pleasure in attending meetings at the Café Royal of a luncheon club organized by Major Alley* for selected members of the S.I.S. and M.I.5. So that their gatherings would not be conspicuous, members of the club going to the Café Royal would stop their taxis two or three blocks away and walk the remaining distance!

While Reilly was enjoying the luxuries of the West End, an impoverished eighteen-year-old student at the St. John's Wood Art School was helping her mother to run a boarding-house for social misfits. Introverted as a child and not blessed with good health, she had been baptized a Catholic by her agnostic mother and had developed into something of a mystic. Through her powers of extra-sensory perception, she had seen a 'vision' in 1918, foretelling the death of the Tsar. She wrote:

I was on my way to buy potatoes. Suddenly, I was held still, as if a magnet held my feet to a particular spot in the middle of the road. In front of me, above me, literally wiping out not only the grey street and

* Major Alley handed over his position as head of the Russian section of the S.I.S. in 1919 to Boyce after which he joined M.I.5.

sky but the whole world, was something which I can only call a gigantic and living Russian icon . . . It was an icon of Christ the King crucified.

Not long after, she read in the newspapers of the Tsar's assassination and was shattered to see from press photographs that the face of the Tsar and that seen in her 'vision' were the same:

I had a premonition of things that were to come, of the vast stretch and anguish of the passion of Christ in which Kings of the world, the hierarchies and the common people would be one, in one terrible glory.

This mystical experience – and she was to have several more in the course of her life – drew the young Caryll Houselander, descendant of Samuel Butler and of a Dutch pirate who was hanged in chains, into an ecstatic love affair with Sidney Reilly.

It was one of Caryll's fellow students who came to know Reilly through her acquaintance with one or two Russian *émigrés*, and spoke casually to him of the sensitive young art student, living in such poverty, who was so attracted to Russia. Reilly, whose compassion was easily roused, asked to see some of Caryll's drawings but Caryll was, at first, too shy to bring them. Later, after Reilly had bought a number of her drawings through the intermediary of her girl-friend, Caryll was persuaded to meet him.

For Caryll, it was a case of love at first sight. It seemed to her that Reilly was 'little less than God himself', that he had come 'straight from heaven'. Undoubtedly, Reilly meant a great deal more to Caryll than she did to him, but his love for her was perhaps the most spiritual of his life. There was, at first, nothing sexual in their relationship and, with the approval of Caryll's mother, Reilly gave her the financial help she urgently needed to continue her studies. This he did by subterfuge, pretending that he had sold pictures for her. He derived deep pleasure from discussing comparative religion with her and introduced her to the doctrines of Buddhism, the Jewish faith and the Russian Church which, in spite of her Catholic upbringing, she longed to join.

However, their relationship could not remain for long on such a spiritual level. With her long straight hair – a flaming red, like Margaret's – cut in a fringe across her forehead, Caryll had something of the appearance of a medieval saint. Reilly was attracted by her and Caryll, young and hungry for love, was overcome by a temptation which, she said, swept over her 'as dry grass is swept by a flame of fire'. Moreover, she was only following the example of her art school friends.

Although Reilly never took Caryll with him on his trips abroad, she was an essential part of his life in London.

Reilly, however, was still preoccupied with the problem of staging a counter-revolution in Russia. If for once he had failed in a mission – his 1918 attempt to overthrow Lenin and Trotsky – the second time he would succeed, or rather Savinkoff, with Reilly's help, would succeed.

The British Government also hoped for the overthrow of the Bolsheviks but could not believe that the Soviet system of terrorism and tyranny, unheard of before in history, could last. Despatches reaching the Foreign Office spoke of the operations of the Cheka as 'making the history of the French Revolution and the Spanish Inquisition mild by comparison'. Photographs were unprintable.

By the hundreds and by the thousands, innocent people were tortured and murdered with unbelievable cruelty. The Communists would first strip their victims of their clothes, break their arms and legs, gouge out their eyes and cut off some fingers or a hand before stabbing them all over with a bayonet and smashing in their skulls with hatchets. Men would have their testicles cut off and many women and even school-girls under the age of ten had first to submit to rape.

Other despatches to the Foreign Office told of people having their mouths slit by bayonets and their tongues cut out. Ex-Tsarist officers by the hundred had their shoulder straps nailed to their bodies then, bound naked in barbed wire they would be lowered into holes made in the ice until they froze to death. Countless others were burned alive, buried alive, thrown into wells to drown or placed in slag gas-pits to die of suffocation. Luckier victims were shot or decapitated with a sword. Beards were torn from faces with the flesh on them, hot needles thrust under finger nails. Noses were cut off. Some victims were literally sawn in pieces and given to the dogs in the streets to eat. Even the sick and wounded were taken from hospitals to be hatcheted to death. In Petrograd the canals were full of decomposed bodies and in one month the population of the city fell by 100,000. The situation elsewhere in Russia was little better. Even peasants were murdered when they protested at the requisition of their cattle. Factory workers were shot if they complained about conditions.

Criminals had been loosed from the gaols and made

commissars. In the prisons, innocent, starved and terrorized men, women and young girls were herded together in verminous, ill-ventilated cells with no sanitation. No-one was allowed out except when called for execution.

In Odessa, several hundred officers of the Black Sea Fleet had either been half-killed in boiling steam and then drowned in the sea or tied to planks and pushed inch by inch into the ships' furnaces. The crew of the Bolshevik flagship replaced their officers by taking on board the entire inmates of the two largest brothels in the port.

In some districts in Russia, women were actually 'nationalized' for the benefit of the comrades. A commissar would be given a certificate giving him 'the right to acquire a girl for himself and no-one may oppose this in any way.' Mixed schools were instituted in which pupil 'commissars' sacked their masters and morals disintegrated so completely that venereal disease spread rapidly throughout Russia's school-children.

To reinforce this ghastly reign of terror, disease took a heavy toll of the population. The Red Guards rarely buried their victims but left them to rot where they lay. Typhus, cholera and smallpox were rife.

It is hardly surprising that the main bulk of the Russian people were anti-Bolshevik, but Lenin's policy was not only to break the spirit of the masses by terrorism but, by starvation, to break them in body as well. Those who were not committed Bolsheviks were only allowed a daily ration of ¼ lb. of black bread or ½ lb. of unmilled oats. The starving people were physically incapable of throwing off the yoke of their better fed oppressors.

While the rest of the world was aghast but mostly

stunned into inactivity by the horrors perpetrated in the name of Communism, Reilly vowed he would liberate the Russian people from the Bolshevik monster. And yet in the corridors of Whitehall, there were voices raised against Reilly. The Etonians in the Foreign Office who had neither visited Russia, nor spoke Russian, saw Reilly as an upstart who had no business to meddle in international politics. M.I.5 noted his leftish inclinations. Eyebrows were raised by some, who scarcely knew the difference between a Bolshevik, Menshevik or a Social-Revolutionary, at Reilly's association with and patronage of Savinkoff and the Social-Revolutionaries. It was rumoured that much of the money he had collected to finance his Moscow counter-revolution had stayed in his own pocket.

Above all, some officials were distinctly unhappy about the S.I.S. employing an agent about whom so little was known and yet who seemed to wield such power. Master spy perhaps, but might he not be ready to serve the highest bidder? Might he not be that most dangerous of animals in the jungle of espionage – the double agent?

The seeds of doubt were sown in the mind of even Captain Sir Mansfield Cumming* who, better than anyone, knew the tremendous services Reilly had rendered to Britain. 'C' had the highest regard for Reilly but was as puzzled by him as everyone else who came into contact with the espionage ace. For all his past achievements, Cumming had to consider the secrecy behind which Reilly hid so much of his real self. His almost megalomaniac personality and grandiose ideas were

* Created K.C.M.G. in 1919.

disturbing. His character seemed so full of contradictions; ruthless, yet at times highly emotional and sensitive, he was a man apparently of the highest integrity in his work and in his everyday relationships with his friends, and yet was quite unscrupulous when it came to business. A gambler, a womanizer and an exhibitionist who loved luxury, he was quite unlike the average agent whose private life was usually a secluded one in a suburban backwater. He was a man who committed bigamy and had probably murdered for his own ends. Yet none could doubt his amazing courage.

To Cumming it was not so much a question of whether or not he could continue to depend on Reilly but whether Reilly could trust himself. Cumming feared that the damage to Reilly's pride, which had resulted from the failure of the Moscow plot, was something a man of his character would be unable to withstand. Reilly's hatred of the Bolsheviks was something abnormal; there was a possibility that he would 'crack'. After pondering all the factors involved, Cumming decided that Reilly's reliability and, therefore, his future usefulness would have to remain in doubt.

It was at this time that Reilly applied to 'C' to be formally enrolled on the permanent staff of M.I.1C. This was a strange request. Through his espionage career it was Reilly who had always insisted on the loose arrangements which had existed between him and the Secret Intelligence Service. He had nearly always preferred to work when and where he chose, frequently without remuneration. In fact, since the débâcle of Moscow, Reilly badly needed to have his self-confidence restored. However, since Cumming was having doubts about his future usefulness, his application for permanent enrolment into the S.I.S. was ill-timed. As tactfully as he could Cumming pointed out to Reilly that he was now a marked man; he was Bolshevism's public enemy No. 1; his photograph had been circulated to Russian agents throughout the world, and his usefulness as a spy impaired. Cumming told him that he would undoubtedly be of sterling value to M.I.1C. in the years to come but that in the existing circumstances it would be better if the loose arrangements which had always existed between him and the department were to continue.

It would be an understatement to say that Reilly took the decision badly. The apparently sinister, ruthless man of unrivalled courage was heart-broken and Cumming later said it was the most painful interview he had ever had. And yet Reilly, who so much wanted to return to Russia, was not jealous of Paul Dukes who had been sent by Cumming to Russia at the end of 1918 and who had been doing magnificent work there for the S.I.S. Indeed, when Dukes was summoned to Cumming for his first interview with the Secret Service Chief, Reilly was present at the meeting and endorsed Cumming's selection* of him to go to Russia for the S.I.S. Dukes and Reilly became good friends.

Reilly appealed to Bruce Lockhart for help. To him he wrote:

---

* Cumming, in fact, nearly turned down Dukes. However, towards the end of the interview, Dukes expressed an interest in the collection of fire-arms which Cumming kept in the office. It was Dukes' sketchy knowledge of pistols rather than his intimate familiarity with Russia which got him the job. Cumming later said: 'But for Paul's interest in my fire-arms I might never have taken on one of my very best agents!' Whereas Reilly's code-name was 'S.T.1', that of Dukes was 'S.T.25'.

I told 'C' (and I am anxious that you should know it too) that I consider that there is a very earnest obligation upon me to continue to serve – if my services can be made use of in the question of Russia and Bolshevism. I feel that I have no right to go back to the making of dollars until I have discharged my obligations. I also venture to think that the state should not lose my services. I would devote the rest of my wicked life to this kind of work. 'C' promised to see the F.O. about all this.

I need not enlarge upon my motives to you; I am sure you will understand them and if you can do something I should feel grateful. I should like nothing better than to serve under you.

I don't believe that the Russians can do anything against the Bolsheviks without our most active support. The salvation of Russia has become a most sacred duty which we owe to the untold thousands of Russian men and women who have sacrificed their lives because they trusted in the promise of our support.

Was Cumming's decision about Reilly the right one? If Cumming ever doubted the wisdom of his decision there was certainly no doubt about its effect on Reilly. His hatred of the Bolsheviks increased tenfold. From that moment on, Reilly had but one goal in life which he never abandoned. In his own words, it was 'to give up my life to Russia to help rid her from this slavery, that she may be a free nation'. Almost alone in a world which was awe-struck by the mere mention of Bolshevism, Reilly tried to organize and bring to fruition the chaotic counter-revolutionary movements which were springing up in Western Europe. His courage and tenacity never failed.

The world of foreign politics is a hard one and that of espionage still harder and it will be seen later how the British Secret Service exploited Reilly's talents and dedication for its own purposes. In all probability had Cumming agreed that day to give Reilly the 'status symbol' for which he asked, Reilly's life might have taken a very different turn. He was certainly an enigma but had Cumming known something more of his childhood and background, he would perhaps have understood the motivating force behind all Reilly's actions and the secrecy with which he surrounded his past. Leonardo da Vinci was a bastard and a genius. Reilly was something of a genius in his own way too and such men should be carefully handled. Had Cumming acceded to Reilly's request, there would have been plenty of ways of dispensing with his services if Cumming had later felt the decision to be wrong. Had he ordered Reilly to an assignment which had no connection with Russia, he might perhaps have diverted his talents and energies into other channels. His anti-Bolshevik crusading spirit might have been damped down and his services employed in other fields for many years. All this, however, is speculation. What is certain is that henceforward Reilly did devote himself with untiring energy to an anti-Bolshevik crusade. The loose arrangement between him and M.I.1C. continued.

In Poland, France, Czechoslovakia and in various parts of Russia itself groups of both White Russians and Social-Revolutionaries were either actively resisting the Bolsheviks or discussing means of doing so. But the absence of co-ordination among the different counter-revolutionary factions was complete.

The British Government despatched a mission and supplies to South Russia in an attempt to support the White Russian troops which, first under General Denikin and later under General Wrangel, were still fighting the Bolsheviks. On Reilly's advice, Cumming sent Hill to South Russia to try to achieve some degree of co-ordination among the White Russian intelligence organizations. All British efforts were in vain and in the end, to save them from annihilation by Red execution squads, some 250,000 Whites were evacuated and settled in Western Europe. Denikin was a good soldier but he was hopelessly handicapped by the right-wing politicians in his entourage.

On the instructions of Cumming, Hill was reporting from South Russia to Reilly, who, both in London and in Paris, was maintaining contact with all the main anti-Bolshevik movements. It was obvious to Reilly that if the various factions were to be welded together, a strong leader was essential. Although he saw himself in such a role, he had enough sense to see that what was needed was a politician or soldier whose name commanded more or less universal respect among anti-Bolshevik Russians. No-one fitted the bill exactly but Boris Savinkoff seemed the only sensible choice.

Winston Churchill, a passionate advocate of intervention, was much impressed by Boris Savinkoff, to whom Reilly had introduced him. He agreed with Reilly that Savinkoff was a man of greater stature than any of the other Russian expatriates and that he was the one man who might organize a successful counter-revolution. There were others who thought themselves qualified for the task but most were primarily hoping to obtain Government funds which they could appropriate for their personal use.

Savinkoff, the former Minister for War under Kerensky and the hero of the Yaroslavl engagement of 1918, was in his forties. A small dark man, slightly bald, he was a heavy smoker and a morphine addict. To many, including Winston Churchill, he appeared a brave and resolute man. Somerset Maugham, who had been in Russia during the war, was also among his admirers. His enemies branded him a coward who showed courage only under the influence of drugs. It was said of him that although he had organized thirty-three assassination plots, including the murder of the Tsar's uncle, the Grand Duke Serge, he had never dared throw a bomb himself. Nevertheless, from among a poor group of candidates, he was probably the best potential leader of a counter-revolution and it was in the Savinkoff boat that Reilly nailed his flag to the mast.

If Reilly ever had doubts about Savinkoff, they were dispelled by the praise and admiration which his own great hero, Churchill, accorded to the Social-Revolutionary leader.

IX

He that hath no stomach to this fight,
Let him depart; his passport shall be made.

HENRY V

With Churchill's blessing and with the qualified support of the British Secret Service chiefs, Reilly was now to champion Savinkoff's cause throughout the world. He did so first in France and in Poland in which there were now large numbers of White Russian refugees. From the French Government came the money which was essential if the counter-revolution was to have a chance of success.

In 1920, Poland and Russia were at war and the Poles were waging fierce guerrilla warfare against the Bolsheviks behind the Russian lines. Savinkoff and Reilly therefore went to Poland and so did Sir Paul Dukes.* In Warsaw the three men held counsel with Colonel Bahalovich, a modern Robin Hood, who led a large band of guerrillas consisting mainly of White Russians.

Bahalovich stole arms, food and money where he could to continue the fight, but the important thing was that he was killing Bolsheviks. A supply of arms and funds was organized for Bahalovich, while Reilly,

* Created K.B.E. for his Secret Service work in Russia in 1919.

Dukes and Savinkoff together toured the White Russian contingents exhorting them to keep up the struggle. Under the protection of Savinkoff's friend, Marshal Pilsudsky, insurrections among the peasants of South Russia were fostered.

Another of Reilly's main contacts in Warsaw was a British Secret Service agent called Maclaren. He was an ex-merchant navy man and the gold ear-rings which he sometimes wore in his pierced ears, gave him the look of a pirate. Maclaren was an ardent worker in the anti-Bolshevik cause and he was Reilly's main funnel for the distribution of funds to the counter-revolutionaries in Poland.

In the summer of 1921, Reilly and Savinkoff organized a secretly convened 'Anti-Bolshevik Congress' in Warsaw to which delegates with differing shades of political opinion were invited, including a number of anti-Reds from within Russia itself. Savinkoff was President of the Congress. Although most of the delegates were Social-Revolutionaries, there was an attempt, although abortive, to establish a working liaison with the White Russian elements loyal to the ex-Tsarist General Wrangel. Reilly attended the first session of the three-day 'Congress' but when it was clear that all plans would come to nought without proper finance, he hurriedly left for Prague to seek more funds.

While Reilly's main British contact in Warsaw was Maclaren of the S.I.S., Savinkoff's link-man in Poland was D. V. Filosofoff. It was Filosofoff who was instructed by the Congress to report the results to Reilly. He wrote Reilly as follows:

I will tell you frankly that I felt ashamed to associate with people who had come to attend and would return to Russia full of hope and would risk their lives in their work – whereas we were unable to give them help to continue to struggle.

I repeat for the um-teenth time that it all depends on money. The press is ready, the peasants await liberation but without a fully planned organization, it is hopeless. Our chief trouble is that it may not be possible to prevent abortive or premature riots. This applies especially to Petrograd from whence we received detailed intelligence (after your departure). From this we see that riots can be expected at any moment and, if they cannot be supported, it is possible that they will be suppressed. Even Boris Savinkoff will not be able to go there owing to insufficient financial aid. In other words – money, money, money!

I am able to say that if the Central Committee issues general marching orders, we can then count on twenty-eight districts including Petrograd, Smolensk and Gomel. Further, the Ukrainians have joined us and have agreed to act in co-ordination. We have contacts with about ten other Governments in outlying districts.

Optimism, as Reilly was continually finding out, was no substitute for organization and money. Nevertheless, his own optimism and efforts to achieve order and raise funds were untiring.

The holding of the 'Anti-Bolshevik Congress' in Warsaw came to the ears of the Kremlin and soon afterwards, Filosofoff was writing Reilly another letter, sounding an ominous note:

Dear Friend Sidney Georgevich,

I am sending you several more documents including a letter from Chicherin to H. A. Maslovsky and his reply. I am very much afraid that the provoked Bolsheviks will now go to extremes and demand the liquidation of all of us.

Yours in spirit,
D. Filosofoff.

Reilly's roving role took him more and more often to Paris where Savinkoff had established his headquarters. Other friends who formed important strands in the web he was weaving also gravitated to Paris. Sasha Grammatikoff had escaped from Russia and now lived in the Rue Ranelagh. Major Field-Robinson, whose friendship with Reilly has already been mentioned, was there, in charge of the S.I.S. Paris office. The work of Ernest Boyce who looked after Russian matters at S.I.S. headquarters in London took him frequently to the French capital.

In Paris too, Reilly had the pleasure of meeting Fred Astaire, whose brilliant dancing had enthralled him in 1916. The champagne flowed as dancer and spy drank toasts to each other at Maxime's.

With his marriage to Nadine effectively at an end, Reilly was soon deep in another love affair. At forty-seven, Reilly was still as irresistible as ever to women both young and old and the twenty-three-year-old French actress who now came under the spell of his charm was no exception. It was a romance full of fire and passion but the young lady, who was not only beautiful but also intelligent and well-educated, wanted marriage. This did not suit Reilly who already had two wives in Margaret and Nadine and his refusal to marry her was understandable. When she became pregnant and, in tears, once more begged him to marry her, Reilly had no alternative but to refuse again and meet the cost of an abortion. The young actress, not content with the role of mistress, broke off her association with Reilly and it was he who then collapsed in tears in his hotel in the Rue Castiglione. Within a few years, the young lady who might have been the third Mrs. Reilly became a star and a household name in France.

Reilly went to his old friend Sasha Grammatikoff for consolation. Together the two friends would lunch nostalgically near the Madeleine at LaRue's, which was now being run by the former *maître d' hôtel* of Kuba's who had escaped from Petrograd. Grammatikoff, who had arranged Nadine's divorce so that she and Reilly could marry, now put Reilly in touch with French lawyers that they might divorce. Legally, a divorce was unnecessary as the marriage had been bigamous in the first place. Reilly, however, was determined that Nadine remain unaware of his marriage to Margaret and in any event he could scarcely confess to bigamy. As a parting present he gave her a beautiful and valuable collection of jade.

Later, Nadine married Gustav Nobel of the Swedish Nobel Prize family. She died in Switzerland soon after at the end of the 1939–45 war, ignorant to the last of Margaret's existence.

However much he became involved with women, Reilly's work always came first. He would visit one European capital after another, sometimes with and sometimes without Savinkoff, seeking supporters or funds for the counter-revolution. As most of the reports coming out of Russia indicated that the Russian people were far from happy under their new Bolshevik masters, he was optimistic that the régime would soon be overthrown.

Full of plans to raise a peasants' revolt in Russia, Reilly and Savinkoff made several visits to Prague to solicit the financial support of the Czechs. To Bruce Lockhart, in Prague at the time, it seemed that Reilly was now the real leader to whom Savinkoff played second fiddle. Funds from the Czechs were forthcoming and years later, in 1948, in order to discredit the name of Masaryk with the Czech people, the Russians published a book called *Documents on the anti-peoples and anti-national politics of T. G. Masaryk*, which revealed a plot between President Masaryk and Savinkoff to kill Lenin: 200,000 roubles were alleged to have changed hands. Although the book contains a number of outright lies, it reveals a good deal of the truth and shows how closely Bolshevik agents were following every move of the counter-revolutionaries.

An amusing anecdote is told of one of Reilly's visits to Prague. While in the Czech capital he entertained several of the staff of the British Legation to luncheon. Over some excellent food and wine he talked for once about himself and admitted that he was born near Odessa. At the luncheon was a young secretary who had that morning been arranging a visa for Reilly. He had seen Reilly's passport.

'How comes it, Mr. Reilly,' he asked across the table, 'that your passport gives your birthplace as Tipperary when you just said you were born near Odessa?'

Reilly laughed. 'I came to Britain to work for the British. I had to have a British passport and needed a British place of birth and, you see, from Odessa it's a long, long way to Tipperary!'

Among the admirers of Savinkoff that Reilly met

about this time was Brigadier-General Edward Spears, C.B., C.B.E., M.C.,* who had been head of the British Military Mission in Paris at the end of the First World War. The general, who had retired from the army in 1920, had turned to business. Although he was later to establish himself firmly in the forefront of the British business community, at that time he was very inexperienced in commercial matters. When, in recognition for his war services to the Czechs, he was offered the chance to handle the radium of which Czechoslovakia was then the only producer, it was Reilly who helped and advised him in Prague. In General Spears' own words: 'Reilly accompanied me in the capacity of an able businessman which I certainly was not myself at the time.'

General Spears, who had no idea of his business mentor's connections with the Secret Intelligence Service, was astonished to learn from Reilly of his service on the German General Staff during the war. He was impressed not only by Reilly's intelligence but also by his great generosity to the *émigré* Russian musicians in the restaurants of Prague.

In Prague, Reilly usually stayed at the Passage Hotel and was also a frequent visitor to the 'Chapeau Rouge' a hotel-cum-night-club, where over a glass of slivovich he would talk philosophy with Eleanor Toye who, with the cover job of a singer, was now working for Cumming in central Europe. She was afterwards to become Reilly's secretary in London.

By this time, Reilly's bank balance was dwindling fast. He had been living in sumptuous style in half the

---

* Later Major-General Sir Edward Spears, Bart., K.B.E., C.B., M.C., Chairman of Ashanti Goldfields and President of the Institute of Directors.

capitals of Europe; Margaret and Nadine had cost him a pretty penny. A considerable sum was due to him from the Baldwin Locomotive Company of the United States, by way of commission on war supplies purchased for the Tsarist Government, but payment was being delayed.

Above all, despite financial aid from the French, Polish and Czech Governments, Savinkoff and his entourage were always in need of extra funds. Reilly was continually dipping into his own pocket to help them. He drew no money from the Secret Service and little was coming in from other sources. Generous to a fault, he frequently lent money to personal friends who were having a hard time after the war; it was not usually repaid.

In London, Reilly openly made contact with Krassin, the Soviet representative to the British Government. Reilly made out that he was no longer interested in anything but business and the Soviet representative was not above making money himself.

Although M.I.5, were very keen at this time to get near Krassin, even Major Alley could get little out of Reilly about his 'business' with Krassin. The Soviet representative was, in fact, putting away in his own bank account funds which the Kremlin leaders were slowly building up abroad for use should they ever have to flee from Russia. When the Kremlin discovered Krassin's fraud, he was recalled to Moscow and 'died' soon afterwards. What the Communists did not know was that Reilly, in turn, had swindled Krassin out of some of the Red funds which he then passed on to Savinkoff for the counter-revolutionaries!

Savinkoff and his entourage were always hard put to it to make ends meet and in June, 1921, Reilly received the following S.O.S. letter from Maclaren in Warsaw:

The position is becoming desperate. The balance in hand today amounts to 700,000 Polish Marks, not even sufficient to pay the staff their salaries for the month of July.

Savinkoff, who is wanted in Finland urgently in order to bring the Petrograd organizations into line and keep them from starting the revolution prematurely, cannot go there, not having the wherewithal to pay for his journey.

Reilly's finances could not stand the strain of supporting Savinkoff for ever. He moved out of the Albany and into a flat at 5, Adelphi Terrace, W.C.2. From here he combined his work for Savinkoff with a renewed interest in business. He dealt in chemicals, pharmaceutical products and once again in patent medicines. With enthusiasm he tried to market a pill to cure baldness.

Reilly's knowledge of Europe inevitably brought him in touch with the merchant bankers in the City of London. For Herbert Wagg & Co., he went to Czechoslovakia to negotiate the Prague Loan, which was subject to tender. By subterfuge and bribery, he learnt the terms offered by all rival bidders before putting in a better bid on behalf of Herbert Wagg. For reasons which the Czech authorities kept to themselves, the loan was nevertheless given to others to handle.

Another important anti-Bolshevik figure was the ex-Prime Minister Alexander Feodorovich Kerensky who had escaped from Russia on a Serbian passport provided by Bruce Lockhart. Kerensky, however, took little direct part in counter-revolutionary activities and could never see eye to eye with Savinkoff. Reilly had several meetings with Kerensky in Prague in 1921 but

his strenuous efforts to patch up the differences between the former Russian Prime Minister and his
former War Minister were to no avail. Indeed Kerensky
accused Reilly of a breach of confidence in mentioning
these discussions at all to anyone. There was little
further contact between Reilly and Kerensky and the
following letter from Reilly evoked no great response:

Passage Hotel, Prague.   21st July, 1921

Dear Alexander Feodorovich,

I was glad that I met you quite by chance today and
to have heard the reason why you did not reply to my
letter of yesterday. You accused me of indiscretion.
In the interest of our work, please tell me what was
the reason for this accusation.

On Tuesday I met V.M.Z.* and told him that I had
visited you and had had a long conversation with
you. The following discussion took place:

q. 'On the same subject which you discussed with
me?'

a. 'Yes, the same.'

q. 'Well, what did you find out? Is A.F.† more
manageable than I am?'

a. 'Yes, I was very pleased with our conversation and
I think that he will reach the desired decision.'

q. 'But don't you think that A.F. was simply being
more diplomatic than me?'

a. 'No, I don't think so. At the beginning of the conversation, we agreed to talk frankly. To talk other-

* Vladimir Mikailovich Zenzinoff, a prominent Social-Revolutionary
and member of the Provisional Government. At this time he was
helping to produce an anti-Bolshevik newspaper in Prague.
† Alexander Feodorovich (Kerensky).

wise would have been a waste of time and I am sure that A.F. considered himself unworthy of playing at diplomacy on such a question at such a critical moment!'

That is all.

We spoke of sabotage in Russia but the name of Savinkoff was never mentioned and I feel sure that V.M.Z. will not refuse to confirm the truth of my statement.

I should be very distressed, if, as a result of this innocent conversation, you were to refrain from finding a means to accomplish the plan I suggested. Even if V.M.Z., for some reason, did not know of our meeting, in what way was it a 'gaffe' to inform him?

The purely practical arrangements on which we both agreed and which, with good management, could help our mutual work, would surely suffer?

I shall contact you on my return from Warsaw and if you wish to see me, I shall be glad to do so.

I hope you will understand the motive of this letter.

Yours very sincerely,
Sidney Reilly.

In the same month Reilly also received an invitation to the First Anti-Bolshevik Congress.

Despite being forced to return to business, Reilly never ceased his efforts to achieve the overthrow of the Soviet Government. He was the driving force behind Savinkoff; and his influence was felt by the counter-revolutionaries who were conspiring behind locked doors in Paris, Prague, Warsaw, Berlin and London.

Helsinki, the Finnish capital, was another important counter-revolutionary centre. The Finnish Government and the Finnish General Staff were mostly anti-Soviet and the main escape route for refugees from Red Russia, a route which came to be known as 'The Window', was across the Russo–Finnish border. Helsinki, at this time, teemed with counter-revolutionaries, spies and counter-espionage agents.

The anti-Reds, however, showed an incapacity for organization equalled only by their capacity for quarrelling among themselves. They were good at talking but quite unable to put a plan into action. In order to avoid absolute chaos, Reilly tried to insist on order but the task was an impossible one. Although the occasional Bolshevik agent would be assassinated, even the good work of Colonel Bahalovich on the Polish–Russian borders had petered out after peace between Poland and Russia was ratified in March, 1921. The Bolshevik secret police, however, now known as the G.P.U.,* the new name which in 1922 Lenin had given to the Cheka, were highly efficient. The Russians were adept in the use of agents-provocateurs even in the days of the Tsar and they now had agents everywhere trying to infiltrate into the counter-revolutionary groups. Reilly had to be constantly on his guard against refugees from Russia who were Bolsheviks in disguise. Eternal vigilance was imperative.

Reilly was untiring in his efforts to stimulate the ruling classes in Britain into backing the counter-revolutionaries and one of his ideas was to try to get his own spokesman in the House of Commons to lead an

---

*Gossudarstyemoye Politicheskoye Upravlyeniye (State Security for Combating Counter-Revolution).

anti-Bolshevik 'lobby'. He suggested to his friend Paul Dukes that he should stand for Parliament and in October, 1922 wrote him the following letter:

You will remember the talks we had before you first went to America and the plans for your future which we were discussing. I refer especially to the idea of your going into Parliament. I have carefully thought about this question since I first heard of your return, and as your return almost coincided with the present political crisis the idea immediately came into my mind: here is Paul Dukes' great chance. What I mean is this: if I were so situated as you seem to me to be I would immediately chuck everything else now, come over to England, get in touch with a Parliamentary organization and forthwith stand for Parliament at the coming elections. You have exceptional advantages: a well-known name, a title, the habit of public speaking, an exceptional knowledge of one of the most burning questions – the Russian question. The title of Paul Dukes, M.P. for Russia is yours for the asking. In the course of next year the Russian question (recognition of the Soviets, British trade with Russia, etc., etc.) will become one of the most vital ones in international politics, and you have the chance of becoming its foremost exponent.

I need not tell you how important it will be for the accomplishment of all our aims to have a man like you in the British Parliament. If my suggestion, which appealed to you when I first made it to you more than a year ago, still appeals to you, then you will probably immediately ask yourself 'what party am I to join?' My reply is the Conservative one. This is the party which is going to carry the majority at the next election, and it is the only one which can give this country sound and purposeful Government inside and outside. Almost instinctively one evokes the bogey of reaction when one talks of Conservatism. I would not be afraid of this. It is REACTION, constructive reaction, which this country and also all the other countries of Europe want after the orgy of destructive radicalism which has been going on now since the war.

This is a question on which I could enlarge indefinitely but I will spare you, as we can talk about it when you have made up your mind and have come here.

Now there is another thing I want to write to you about. I hope you find time to see Savinkoff. His address 32 Rue de Lubeck, and his telephone No. is Passy 95–18. Savinkoff was and is and always will be the only man outside of Russia worth talking to and worth supporting. Everybody else is dead as a doornail. Notwithstanding the enormous persecution to which he has been subjected, notwithstanding the incredible difficulties he has had to contend with, he has kept his organization both here and in Russia alive, and he is the only man amongst the Russian anti-Bolsheviks who is actually working. It is superfluous to tell you that I am sticking to him through thick and thin and that I shall continue to do so until I find a bigger man. It is not a matter of personal friendship or personal admiration, it is simply a case of what is the best way in which I can serve Russia at the present moment.

Sir Paul Dukes would undoubtedly have added to the lustre of the House of Commons, but he had no particular ambition to enter the political arena.

However eager the British Government may have been to see the end of Bolshevism, the Secret Service chiefs were not very optimistic about the chances of success of a counter-revolution. Reilly kept them informed about all the plots and counter-plots with which Europe seethed and, while it was unwilling to commit funds to the counter-revolutionary movement itself, M.I.1C. certainly did not wish to discourage Reilly in his activities. Without committing themselves, the British collected a great deal of valuable intelligence from Reilly.

It was on a visit to Berlin in December, 1922 that Reilly met a charming young actress in the Hotel Adlon. Pepita Bobadilla was an attractive blonde from South America. The widow of Charles Haddon-Chambers, a well-known playwright, she had started her stage career as one of C. B. Cochran's 'young ladies' in the same chorus as Binnie Hale and had played in a number of roles on the London stage. A week after their first meeting they became engaged and although Reilly had to leave her almost immediately, as business for Savinkoff took him for some time to Paris and Prague, the couple were married on May 18th, 1923, at the Covent Garden Registry Office in Henrietta Street. Reilly's old friends Captain George Hill and Major Stephen Alley acted as witnesses. Like Nadine before her, Pepita was completely ignorant of the existence of Margaret. Reilly had contracted another bigamous marriage. Cumming, who knew only too well of the marriage to Margaret, did nothing to prevent this breach of the law by his star agent. He even attended the wedding reception at the Savoy Hotel and congratulated Pepita on her marriage.

Reilly's marriage to Pepita brought to a tragic end his affair with Caryll which had lasted over three years. The anguish of the final separation nearly broke her heart and for consolation she returned to the Catholic Church. She never loved a man again and never married. Her love for Reilly was, henceforth, to find expression in an almost unlimited love for all mankind. She became perhaps the most widely read Catholic writer of the century.* Caryll also developed a talent extraordinary in a laywoman for healing the mentally sick. The late Dr. Eric Strauss, President of the Psychiatry Section of the Royal Society of Medicine, would pass on to her his hopeless cases. He said of her that 'she loved them back to life'. Where doctors and nurses failed she would soothe the troubled minds of violent patients in the padded cells of St. Bernard's Hospital – Britain's largest mental institution. Priests and even the police sought her help.

At the time of his marriage to Pepita, Reilly's personal finances and those of Savinkoff were at a low ebb. Reilly's business ventures had not prospered; he still awaited the money due to him from the United States and, in the absence of any effective moves by the counter-revolutionaries, the French and other Governments had withdrawn their financial support from Savinkoff. Savinkoff, and his staff, bodyguard and numerous agents, who were moving in and out of Russia with surprising ease, badly needed money. For cash, the counter-revolution now had to rely almost entirely on private individuals. Though he was frustra-

* Author of *The Flowering Tree, This War is the Passion, The Reed of God,* etc. For the reader interested in Caryll Houselander there is an excellent biography of her by Maisie Ward published by Sheed & Ward.

ted by the inefficiency of the anti-Soviet governments, Reilly never lost heart. With hardly a word of complaint he sold the greater part of his cherished collection of Napoleana; the fruits of half a lifetime of collecting went to bolster up the Savinkoff coffers.

Some idea of Reilly's relationship with and influence over Boris Savinkoff is seen in a letter which the latter's mother wrote to Reilly about this time. Marked 'Very Private' it was an appeal to Reilly to use his powers to stop her son from fomenting riots in Russia. Madame Savinkova considered these to be a waste of time in view of the lack of funds to sustain them. She wanted Reilly and Savinkoff to concentrate instead on propaganda:

I ask you whether you can guarantee that you will on no account tell Boris that I have written to you. If you cannot, do not continue to read this letter but tear it up. If you agree with my idea and understand its deep meaning you must act independently and not involve me in any way.

Boris values your friendship very much. In his candid moments, he calls you 'a knight without fear or reproach'. He tells me: 'I listen to many but put my faith only in Reilly'; 'he is a tower of moral strength', . . .

In my opinion, the struggle with the Bolsheviks must find another form. It is impossible, sitting in Paris and without a great deal of financial backing, to plan any armed resistance or strike against the present authorities in Russia.

Madame Savinkova then went on to quote a remark of Lloyd George to a friend of hers:

'Savinkoff is no doubt a man of the future but I need Russia at the present moment, even if it must be the Bolsheviks. Savinkoff can do nothing at the moment, but I am sure he will be called on in time to come. There are not many Russians like him.'

I also think so, Sidney Georgevich, and that Boris' part in Russia is not at present . . . Your friendship and energy is essential to prevent Boris being sucked into the web which is gradually forming around him.

It is a question of a newspaper. Boris should perhaps be head of an opposition newspaper. He is a good organizer and you are an excellent administrator. As regards our co-workers, i.e. those who are at present without work, Filosofoff remains in Warsaw as advisor on the Polish situation. Victor Savinkoff, who has done very well, should be sent as a scout somewhere near the Russian frontier, such as Danzig – others like Shevchenko should co-operate, Derenthal is a talented writer and I can be the cashier (ideal, as not a cent will then be wasted!).

I am sure that friends of Boris will subscribe. Then again, if the paper will stress the necessity for 'Saving the Jews' – since there is a strong anti-Jewish movement in Russia and, especially, in Poland – most banks in the hands of the Jews will certainly subscribe . . .

You have a very great influence. I do not know how you will view my suggestion. It seems clear to me that this would be a way out of a critical situation.

There was a good deal of common sense in Madame Savinkova's suggestion and, indeed, several anti-Bolshevik papers in various languages were organized in Europe. Reilly, however was more interested in positive anti-Red activity and continued to apply himself to the difficult task of fund-raising to make a counter-revolution a practical possibility.

By July, 1923, desperate for cash, Reilly decided to go to America where his lawyers were making little progress in settling his claim against the Baldwin Locomotive Company. He booked passages to New York for himself and Pepita in the Holland-Amerika liner *Rotterdam* but as he had no money for the tickets he asked for help from his S.I.S. friend and colleague Major W. Field-Robinson who had returned from Paris to London.

'Robbie,' he said, 'I am broke. My credit in London is finished. I must get over to New York to fight my case. It is my last chance. Will you help?'

'How much do you want?'

'Two hundred pounds,' replied Reilly. 'I have booked our passages, and I haven't the money to pay for them. I need it at once.'

Field-Robinson took Reilly straight to his bank, drew out two £100 notes and handed them to Reilly. He never saw the money again but years later, when commenting on this incident, he said:

'I have never regretted it because he was really a very great friend of mine and helped me get jobs.* I am

---

* Major Field-Robinson was later reduced to part-time work for the S.I.S. and was attached to the Société Française pour le Commerce des Tabacs in the Rue Mogador in Paris as cover for his activities. This was the French subsidiary of the Tobacco Company Ltd., a British company in which Major Alley held a leading post. Alley used the company and its offices abroad to provide cover in Europe for S.I.S. agents and ex-employees of the Secret Service. Hill and later Boyce were also employed by the company. Field-Robinson obtained this post as a result of an introduction from Reilly to Major Alley.

quite certain that had he lived he would have repaid me tenfold in due course. I repeat, I have never regretted the money one instant.'

In New York, Reilly made his headquarters at the Gotham Hotel, selling the last few pieces of Napoleana he had retained. He had never refused a loan to anyone in need but he was now himself forced to borrow money while his lawyers continued to make little headway in his case against Baldwins.

It was a complicated case. When Tsarist rule came to its unhappy end in Russia, the Tsarist Government contracts for purchasing arms and munitions in the United States, for many of which Reilly had been responsible, were taken over by the British Government. One such contract was with the Baldwin Locomotive Company with which Reilly had a commission arrangement. Under a written agreement, Reilly was due commission totalling some $500,000. The British Government, however, when it took over the American contracts, did so only on condition that no commission agreements to third parties existed. Mr. Vanclaim, head of Baldwin's, had therefore asked Reilly to destroy the agreement while giving him his personal assurance that the commission would nevertheless be paid even if it had to come out of his own pocket. Reilly, accepting Vanclaim's word, had torn up the agreement. Vanclaim had made various excuses for delaying payment and now refused to pay at all. Reilly filed a lawsuit against him. Vanclaim continued with his delaying tactics and for the best part of a frustrating twelve months, Reilly stayed in New York, waiting for the case to come before the courts.

Throughout this time, Reilly was in regular communication with Savinkoff in Paris and kept in close personal touch with Savinkoff's sympathizers in New York. He kept watch too on the increasing number of Bolshevik agents reaching America. The G.P.U. likewise kept constant watch on Reilly.

Impatient to return to Europe and resume his struggle against the Red enemy, Reilly felt there was little he could effectively do until he once again had ample funds to inject into the counter-revolutionary movement. To pass the time he helped Sir Paul Dukes, who was lecturing in America at the time, to translate into English Savinkoff's book *The Black Horse*. But all the time his restless brain was devising plans to overthrow the Soviet Government.

In view of what was to happen later, some highly confidential remarks Reilly made to Sir Paul Dukes at this time were of considerable significance. One day in New York he turned to Dukes and, *à propos* of nothing at all, said:

'I am going to tell you something very, very, private. I am not telling anyone else and no-one must know. Savinkoff is going back to Russia to give himself up. I too am going back but I shall continue to fight.'

Reilly would say no more, but we shall return to these remarks shortly.

Meanwhile Reilly's case against Baldwin continued to be delayed and when, in the summer of 1924, Reilly received an urgent summons to Paris from Savinkoff, he did not hesitate to return to Europe. Pepita accompanied him, but before his departure Reilly made certain financial arrangements in New York to take care of her in the event of his death. He was clearly anticipating a return to Russia and the danger that this would entail.

On arrival in Paris, Reilly found that Savinkoff was

away in Rome, seeking the financial support of Mussolini. From Dehrenthal, Savinkoff's personal assistant, he heard of the important developments to which Savinkoff had referred in his correspondence.

Reference has been made to the ease with which Savinkoff's agents were passing in and out of Russia. These agents were bringing back reports of a strong anti-Bolshevik movement which had been built up inside Russia and which included many men in high places, including some in the G.P.U. itself. The organization was known as the Moscow Municipal Credit Association but was commonly called 'The Trust'. Its active leaders included a man called Yakushev and another called Opperput. Both Pavlovsky, Savinkoff's principal contact in Moscow, and the White Russian General Kutyepoff, who headed an anti-Soviet combat group formed in Finland, had complete faith in 'The Trust'. It was through the power of 'The Trust' that agents of Savinkoff and General Kutyepoff had been able to cross the Russian frontier through 'The Window' with little risk and to travel about Russia with comparative freedom. Savinkoff and his closest associates had been much impressed both by accounts of 'The Trust's' organization, brought by its messengers, and by the messengers themselves. 'The Trust' was ready to stage a counter-revolution; it lacked only a real leader, such as Savinkoff or Reilly himself, and wanted to be assured of the support of the anti-Bolshevik movement outside Russia. The possibility that the whole story was an ingenious plot of G.P.U. agents-provocateurs to lure the counter-revolutionary leaders into exposing the extent of their own organizations was naturally considered. Reilly was well aware of the deception and endless doublecrossing of which

Bolshevik agents were capable.

All this Reilly had learnt in New York from letters and messengers Savinkoff had sent to him. Furthermore, he was impressed by what he had learnt at first hand from two of 'The Trust's' agents, one of whom had been a spy for Reilly himself in 1918. He saw the chance at last to return to Russia and avenge the failure of the 1918 plot. That he had determined in any event to return to Russia is clear from the remarks he had made to Sir Paul Dukes in New York before these conversations even took place. Nevertheless he was wary: he was too old a hand at the game and knew that many agents were taking pay from both sides. In particular, he was highly sceptical of Savinkoff's plan to go to Russia to give himself up in return for the promise of a fake trial – a trial at which he would confess to his 'anti-Soviet crimes' but would nevertheless be released.

Savinkoff returned from Rome empty-handed. There had been a clash of personalities at his meeting with Mussolini. The most the Duce would do was to provide him with an Italian passport and promise him assistance, if need be, from the Italian Legation in Russia.

Savinkoff appeared to have great faith in the powers of 'The Trust'. Disappointment at the outcome of his talks with Mussolini, the continual struggle for funds and, more particularly, the inevitable effects of his long addiction to morphine, had left their mark. Savinkoff was a broken and dispirited man. He grasped at the straw offered by 'The Trust's' proposal. He would return to Russia, 'confess' and turn Bolshevik. To the outside world, he might appear a traitor to his cause but in reality he would be a traitor within the

Red camp, maintain contact with 'The Trust' leaders and be ready to assume leadership when the counter-revolution occurred. Reilly and General Kutyepoff could continue the struggle from outside Russia.

Reilly sought the advice of Ernest Boyce who was now working in Europe for the Russian section of the S.I.S. Boyce confirmed that 'The Trust' was apparently a movement of considerable power within Russia. Its agents had supplied valuable intelligence to the Secret Services of a number of Western European countries. On the other hand, some intelligence had been received which was suspect and which might have been deliberately planted by the G.P.U. The British Secret Service was very anxious to make an accurate assessment of 'The Trust's' real strength.

Although alive to the possibility that agents-provocateurs might be at work, Reilly was still impressed by 'The Trust'. But Savinkoff's plan to go to Russia he considered utter madness. If it was no more than a G.P.U. plot to entice Savinkoff into Red hands, the whole counter-revolutionary movement would suffer a major reverse. For several days he argued strenuously with Savinkoff, urging him not to go, but to no avail.

On August 10th, 1924, Savinkoff, Dehrenthal and his wife, together with two messengers of 'The Trust' left for Russia, via Berlin. Reilly was never to see the former Russian Minister of War again.

The first news came from *Izvestia* on August 29th, which contained a brief report that Savinkoff had been arrested in Russia. Announcements followed rapidly; he had been condemned to death; sentence had been commuted to ten years' imprisonment; he had been completely acquitted; he was a free man.

The powers of 'The Trust' did indeed seem great.

While Reilly was thankful that Savinkoff had not been liquidated, he was greatly perturbed at the unanimous conclusion of the world's press that Savinkoff had thrown in his lot with the Bolsheviks. The effect on the morale of anti-Bolsheviks everywhere would be considerable.

Although propaganda was not one of Reilly's particular talents he sat down and wrote a long letter to the *Morning Post* which was published on September 8th, 1924:

Sir:

My attention has been drawn to the article, *Savinkoff's Nominal Sentence*, published in the *Morning Post* of September 1st. Your informant, without adducing any proofs whatsoever and basing himself merely on rumours, makes the suggestion that Savinkoff's trial was a 'stunt' arranged between him and the Kremlin clique, and that Savinkoff had already for some time contemplated a reconciliation with the Bolsheviks.

No more ghastly accusation could be so carelessly hurled against a man whose whole life has been spent fighting tyranny of whatsoever denomination, Tsarist or Bolshevist, and whose name all over the world has stood for 'No Surrender' to the sinister powers of the Third International.

I claim the great privilege of being one of his most intimate friends and devoted followers, and on me devolves the sacred duty of vindicating his honour. Contrary to the affirmation of your correspondent, I was one of the very few who knew of his intention to penetrate into Soviet Russia. On receipt of a cable from him, I hurried back, at the beginning of July, from New York, where I was assisting my friend, Sir Paul Dukes, to translate and to prepare for publication Savinkoff's latest book, *The Black Horse*. Every page of it is illuminated by Savinkoff's transcendent love for his country and by his undying hatred of the Bolshevist tyrants. Since my arrival here on July 19th, I have spent every day with Savinkoff up to August 10th, the day of his departure for the Russian frontier. I have been in his fullest confidence, and all his plans have been elaborated conjointly with me. His last hours in Paris were spent with me.

Nineteen days later came the news of his arrest, then in quick, almost hourly, succession, of his trial, his condemnation to death, the commutation of the death sentence to ten years' imprisonment, his complete acquittal, and finally his liberation.

Where are the proofs of all this phantasmagoria? What is the source of this colossal libel? The Bolshevist news agency *Rosta*!

It is not surprising that the statements of the *Rosta*, this incubator of the vilest Bolshevist canards, should be swallowed without demur, and even with joy, by the Communist press, but that the anti-Communist press should accept those palpable forgeries for good currency is beyond comprehension.

I am not yet in a position to offer you definite proofs of this Bolshevist machination to discredit Savinkoff's good name; but permit me to call your attention to the following most significant facts:

1. The *Rosta* states that Savinkoff was tried behind closed doors. We must assume that no correspondents of non-Communist European or American papers were present, otherwise the world would have

already had their account of the proceedings.

2. The official Bolshevist journal, the *Izvestia*, up to August 28th, does not mention a single word about Savinkoff. Is it likely that having on the 20th achieved such a triumph as the capture of their 'greatest enemy' the Bolsheviks would pass over it in silence during an entire week?

3. What do all the so-called 'sincere confessions and recantations' consist of? Of old political tittle-tattle which has been known for years to every European Chancery and also to the Bolsheviks, and has now been re-hashed for purposes of defamation and propaganda. Not a single new and really confidential fact as regards Savinkoff's activities or relations with Allied statesmen during the last two years has come to light.

4. No confederates are either mentioned or implicated in the trial with Savinkoff.

What are the inferences to be drawn from all the above facts? Savinkoff was killed when attempting to cross the Russian frontier and a mock trial, with one of their own agents as chief actor, was staged by the Cheka in Moscow behind closed doors.

Need one mention the trials of the Social-Revolutionaries, of the Patriarch, of the Kieff professors, in order to remind the public of what unspeakable villainies the Bolsheviks are capable? For the moment they have succeeded in throwing a shadow on the great name of their admittedly most active and most implacable enemy. But the truth will penetrate even the murky darkness of this latest Cheka conspiracy, and will shine forth before the world. Then it will be seen that of all men who in our time have combated the Moscow tyrants, none had a greater right to

Victor Hugo's proud assertion: *S'il n' en reste qu'un – je le suis!*

Sir, I appeal to you, whose organ has always been the professed champion of anti-Bolshevism and anti-Communism, to help me vindicate the name and honour of Boris Savinkoff.

Yours, etc.
Sidney Reilly

Reilly was particularly concerned at the possible effect of Savinkoff's return to Russia on the opinion of Winston Churchill, who had always championed Savinkoff and who, Reilly was convinced, would eventually persuade the British Government to give full support to a counter-revolution, once this could be shown to have a reasonable chance of success. He therefore wrote to Churchill as follows:

Dear Mr. Churchill,

The disaster which has overtaken Boris Savinkoff has undoubtedly produced the most painful impression upon you. Neither I nor any of his intimate friends and co-workers have so far been able to obtain any reliable news about his fate. Our conviction is that he has fallen a victim to the vilest and most daring intrigue the Cheka has ever attempted. Our opinion is expressed in the letter which I am today sending to the *Morning Post*. Knowing your invariably kind interest I take the liberty of enclosing a copy for your information.

I am, dear Mr. Churchill,
Yours very faithfully,
Sidney Reilly

However, as Winston Churchill was quick to point out, neither in his letter to the *Morning Post* nor in the letter to him, had Reilly explained why Savinkoff had gone to Russia at all. Churchill replied to Reilly's letter as follows:

Chartwell Manor,
Westerham, Kent.
September 5, 1924

Dear Mr. Reilly,

I was deeply grieved to read the news about Savinkoff. I do not, however, think that the explanation in your letter to the Morning Post is borne out by the facts. The Morning Post today gives a fuller account of the procés verbal, and I clearly recognize the points we discussed at Chequers about free Soviet elections, etc. You do not say in your letter what was the reason and purpose with which he entered Soviet Russia. If it is true that he had been pardoned and liberated I should be very glad. I am sure that any influence he could acquire among those men would be powerfully exerted towards bringing about a better state of affairs. In fact their treatment of him, if it is true, seems to me to be the first decent and sensible thing I have ever heard about them.

I shall be glad to hear anything further you may know on the subject, as I always thought Savinkoff was a great man and a great Russian patriot, in spite of the terrible methods with which he has been associated. However it is very difficult to judge the politics in any other country.

Yours very truly,
Winston S. Churchill

Reports which appeared in *Izvestia* later in September seemed to make it clear that Savinkoff had indeed betrayed his cause. This was Savinkoff's 'deception' plan before he left Paris, but Reilly was afraid that Savinkoff was in fact the traitor that he appeared to be.

The Soviet Government 'allowed' Savinkoff to send Reilly a letter from Moscow. In this, S.T.1's old friend wrote:

> Never have I fought for the interests and dubious welfare of Europe, but always for Russia and the Russian people. How many illusions and fairy tales have I buried here in the Loubianka! I have met men in the G.P.U. whom I have known and trusted from my youth up and who are nearer to me than the chatter-boxes of the foreign delegation of the Social-Revolutionaries . . . What does prison mean here? No-one is kept longer than three years and is given leave to visit the town during this time . . . I cannot deny that Russia is reborn.

Reilly was convinced that the letter was a forgery for which Trillisser, the head of the Foreign Section of the G.P.U., was responsible. The G.P.U. maintained a special technical department known as the Kaneva which was extremely adept at 'manufacturing' letters and documents.

To make his own position clear and to rally the depressed anti-Bolshevik cause, Reilly wrote another letter to the *Morning Post*:

> Sir,
>   I once more take the liberty of claiming your indulgence and your space. This time for a twofold

purpose, first of all to express my deep appreciation of your fairness in inserting (in your issue of the 8th inst.) my letter in defence of Boris Savinkoff when all the information at your disposal tended to show that I am in error; secondly, to perform a duty, in this case a most painful duty, and to acknowledge the error into which my loyalty to Savinkoff has induced me.

The detailed and in many instances stenographic press reports of Savinkoff's trial, supported by the testimony of reliable and impartial eyewitnesses, have established Savinkoff's treachery beyond all possibility of doubt. He has not only betrayed his friends, his organization, and his cause, but he has also deliberately and completely gone over to his former enemies. He has connived with his captors to deal the heaviest possible blow at the anti-Bolshevik movement, and to provide them with an outstanding political triumph both for internal and external use. By this act Savinkoff has erased for ever his name from the scroll of honour of the anti-Communist movement.

His former friends and followers grieve over his terrible and inglorious downfall, but those amongst them who under no circumstances will practise with the enemies of mankind are undismayed. The moral suicide of their former leader is for them an added incentive to close their ranks and to carry on.

Yours etc.

Sidney Reilly

Winston Churchill however, did not agree with this verdict and wrote the following letter to Reilly:

September 15, 1924

Dear Mr. Reilly:

I am very interested in your letter. The event has turned out as I myself expected at the very first. I do not think you should judge Savinkoff too harshly. He was placed in a terrible position; and only those who have sustained successfully such an ordeal have a full right to pronounce censure. At any rate I shall wait to hear the end of the story before changing my view about Savinkoff.

Yours very truly,
W. S. Churchill

But Savinkoff had without doubt gone over to the Bolsheviks. His disclosures were not of major importance, but merely sufficient, or so he thought, to convince the G.P.U. that he was a genuine turncoat. 'The Trust' had saved his life. He was treated humanely, but nevertheless kept in confinement, in a 'hotel-prison' in Moscow's Loubianka Square. He was too dangerous a man to be allowed complete freedom. Russian propaganda made the most of his surrender and confessions.

Depressed by his fate, Savinkoff succeeded in smuggling out to Reilly a letter for General Spears asking him to approach Winston Churchill in the hope that the latter could somehow procure his release.

In November, 1924, Filosofoff, who was by now in Paris and who found it impossible to believe that Savinkoff had turned traitor, also received some letters smuggled out of Russia, one of which was from Savinkoff himself. Filosofoff wrote to Reilly:

From these I find (and it is confirmed from other

167

sources) that Savinkoff did not name any of his former associates. On the whole I have the impression that I was right in my first opinion regarding Savinkoff's behaviour.

Filosofoff seemed to pin his hopes for the future on Reilly's ability to get substantial support for a counter-revolution from the United States. Writing to Reilly he drew his attention to 'that strong organization which calls itself "The American Legion" which is preparing a campaign against Bolshevism on a large scale. I do not doubt that with the help of the Americans we shall be able to overthrow the Moscow authorities.'

Eventually Savinkoff committed suicide in May, 1925 by throwing himself out of a window. Contrary to the opinion of many it seems unlikely that his suicide was faked to conceal his death by execution. The G.P.U. certainly had no scruples about murdering its enemies, but on this occasion it would probably have preferred Savinkoff alive. It suited the Russian secret police that Reilly and other leading counter-revolution-aries should continue to believe in the powers of 'The Trust'. In Savinkoff, the Bolsheviks had an implacable enemy under control. Alive, however, he could have served as a bait for the more important enemy – Reilly.

According to the Russian news agency *Rosta*, Savin-koff was writing his memoirs at the time of his suicide. It would be interesting to know what, if anything, he wrote about Reilly.

X

I am about to take my last voyage,
A great leap into the dark.

THOMAS HOBBES

With M.I.1C. still undecided whether or not to support
'The Trust', a policy which Britain's first Labour
Government, then in power, would in any case not
have wanted to adopt, and with Savinkoff no longer
available as an ally, Reilly was once again left to fight
alone. It was a role to which he was quite accustomed
but while he was confident of his ability to deal with
the Soviet Government, he could not do so alone and
without funds. He needed money urgently and since
Savinkoff's return to Russia had discredited the counter-
revolutionary cause, Reilly also needed an event of
major importance to discredit the Bolsheviks and rally
the anti-Reds.

In the early 1920's, a considerable trade had developed in Europe in forged Soviet documents. Governments in Europe were still bemused by the consequences of the Russian Revolution and uncertain of the
attitude they should adopt towards the Kremlin leaders.
Little information came through normal diplomatic
channels and the Secret Services of every country were
eagerly seeking intelligence where ever they could.

This state of affairs placed a premium on intelligence from Russia, true or false. It was a situation in which dealers in forged information thrived.

The I.N.O., or Foreign Department of the G.P.U., was desperately short of foreign currency to support its agents abroad. In addition to the independent forgers who worked for any master or on their own account, the G.P.U. prepared and through its agents abroad sold forged Soviet documents. It even sold genuine documents where these would do no harm to Russia.

The centre of much of this traffic in false Soviet intelligence was Berlin where a black market in forged Soviet documents was established. Agents of various countries bought and sold these forgeries and a number of foreign ministries and intelligence services were deceived by them.

In the European espionage jungle which was his natural habitat, Reilly had his finger on the pulse of this clandestine market in forged documents. He knew that in many cases the forgeries were so expert that no-one except their 'manufacturers' could tell they were not genuine.

Thus it came about that Reilly initiated in England the 'Zinoviev Letter' sensation of October, 1924 which was a major factor in the fall of Ramsay MacDonald's Labour Government.

From his friends and colleagues in London, Reilly knew that a considerable amount of subversive correspondence from the Comintern in Moscow was reaching British Communists. To make public a thoroughly subversive letter to the British Communist Party from Zinoviev himself, the President of the Comintern,*

* The Comintern was formed in 1919 to replace the Second International.

might well rally British public opinion behind the anti-Bolshevik movement. This would boost the morale of anti-Reds everywhere, who were dispirited by Savinkoff's return to Russia.

Zinoviev, a man with cold, calculating eyes and coarse, cruel lips, had been Lenin's companion in exile in Switzerland and was one of his closest friends. He was known to be a bitter enemy of England which he described as 'the country which can never be reconciled with Russia'. A subversive letter from him would be quite in keeping with his known attitude.

Among the sinister dealers in Russian intelligence, true and forged, was Sasha Grammatikoff's friend, Vladimir Orloff, the Public Prosecutor for the Tsar, who had succeeded in joining the Cheka under a false name and who had provided Reilly with his pass in the name of Comrade Relinsky in 1918. Orloff had eventually been forced to flee Russia and had gone to Berlin.

In the German capital, Orloff set up as a free-lance spy working both for the White Russians and for the Germans. One of his associates was a Pole who had also entered the Cheka as a spy. This was Pavlonovsky, alias Sumarokoff, alias Yakschin, alias Karapoff, who had fled Russia in 1922 with a trunkful of stolen Cheka papers which served not only as good currency in the espionage market but also as excellent 'specimens' for subsequent forgeries. Like Orloff, Pavlonovsky also worked for the German Political Police. Yet another associate was Serge Drushilovsky, who had worked as a forger for Trillisser, the head of the G.P.U.'s Foreign Department, and who was in Berlin in 1924.

It was easy for Reilly to explain to Orloff and Pavlonovsky what he wanted. They already possessed both manufactured and real letters which could have served

Reilly's purpose but Reilly insisted on a letter from Zinoviev himself. With the aid of Drushilovsky and some White Russians in Berlin, who could not have foreseen the political uproar it would create in England, the letter was concocted. Orloff and Pavlonovsky,* on instructions from Reilly, who kept to himself his ultimate plan for the letter, concealed their connection with the forgery as far as possible and Reilly's own name was never mentioned to those working on the letter. Reilly was determined that the British should treat the letter as genuine. Much depended on it and he knew that his own reputation with the British Secret Service might be ruined if it was learnt that he had instigated a forgery.

On the question of the morals of passing off a false document as the real thing he had no scruples. It was in a good cause and the letter was no more subversive than many genuine letters from the Comintern.

The Zinoviev Letter, dated September 15th, 1924 and 'signed' by Zinoviev, called on British Communists to organize armed insurrection and subversion in the British armed forces. It referred also to the recruitment of leaders for a future 'Red' British army. Through devious channels, Reilly organized the delivery of the letter to the Foreign Office in London and made sure that it reached the press.

Although Ramsay MacDonald, the Labour Prime Minister, was aware of the contents of the letter, which were kept secret from the public for some time, he

* A few years later Orloff and Pavlonovsky were both given prison sentences in Germany for forging Soviet documents which suggested that certain U.S. Senators were accepting bribes from the Soviet Government. Drushilovsky was shot by the Russians as a traitor for his part in the forgery to which he confessed during his trial by a Soviet court.

continued to boast in his General Election campaign, which was in full swing at the time, of the Labour Government's success in achieving co-operation and understanding with the Russians. When the *Daily Mail* finally revealed the contents of the Zinoviev Letter, Ramsay MacDonald was completely discredited and Labour lost the election. Many Socialists subsequently alleged that the document was a forgery and arguments about its authenticity have continued ever since.

Contrary to a popular theory, there is no reason to believe that Reilly was in any way personally interested in using the Zinoviev Letter to help the Conservatives at the General Election. He probably did not foresee the uproar it would create on the British political scene. Any remuneration he may have received almost certainly went to help the anti-Bolshevik movement.

If the Foreign Office was deceived by the forgery, this was not surprising. The Zinoviev Letter was very similar to many genuine documents of a subversive nature which emanated from Moscow. Don Gregory, then head of the Northern Department at the Foreign Office, consulted Sir Thomas Preston over its authenticity. Preston, who was head of the British Mission in Russia and knew Zinoviev personally, told Gregory he had no doubt that it was genuine.

Reilly made no secret to his close friends of his responsibility for the Zinoviev Letter and Major Alley recalls how pleased he was with this coup. A 1966 Russian publication in an oblique reference to the Zinoviev Letter implies quite clearly that in 1925 Reilly admitted his role in the affair to a Soviet agent-provocateur, unknown as such to Reilly at the time.

Some years later, Reilly's file of papers on the

Zinoviev Letter was stolen, presumably by G.P.U. agents, from Pepita's flat in Paris. And, in an astonishing admission made in December, 1966, the Foreign Office revealed that vital documents relating to the Zinoviev Letter were 'missing' from its own file on the affair.

Soon after the Zinoviev Letter scandal, Reilly crossed over to the United States to resume his fight with Baldwin's. In due course, the case came up before judge and jury. Vanclaim openly admitted the existence of an agreement with Reilly but maintained his legal right to refuse payment, as Reilly had destroyed the agreement. Since the miscarriage of his planned coup of 1918, it seemed to Reilly that all his subsequent moves had achieved little. Whereas nearly all his ventures prior to 1918 had succeeded, since Moscow little had gone right. Now, even his legitimate dues were being denied. In court, Reilly completely lost his self-control: it was the hated Bolsheviks who had caused his ruin. Sir Paul Dukes, who attended the case, says that Reilly's rage in court was ungovernable; he literally foamed at the mouth and saliva dribbled down his chin: 'he was a very ugly sight indeed'. Morally, Reilly was in the right but according to the letter of the law he had no case and his claim was dismissed.

If fury gave way to despondency, it was not for long. He never lost hope and thought it a crime to despair. Like Napoleon, he had failed to take Moscow but he had not yet met his Waterloo. Reilly's determination and courage were unlimited and he soon returned to the fight.

Bolshevik agents were entering the United States in increasing numbers, both as G.P.U. agents-provocateurs and as spies to watch the ever growing, if ineffectual, numbers of White Russians reaching America. The Soviet Government, whose finances were in a poor state, was trying to obtain a major loan from the United States. The rate of interest offered was tempting.

With undiminished zeal Reilly wrote article after article to the press and gave one public lecture after another denouncing the iniquities and horrors of the Soviet régime. He seemed to be winning the battle of wits which he was fighting with the Russian secret police.

The G.P.U. had succeeded in planting an agent in Reilly's New York office in the form of a female secretary. Although he quickly spotted her, he said nothing. For nearly a year, he fed her with fake documents and correspondence of a completely misleading nature, copies of which went straight to Moscow. His real work he did at night after his secretary had gone home. By following up her contacts and those of another known G.P.U. agent, Reilly soon uncovered most of the Bolshevik secret agents operating in New York. The Soviet Government never received their American loan; Reilly's anti-Bolshevik propaganda and his disclosures of G.P.U. spy rings were convincing.

Success seemed to be coming his way once again and although he continued to live for the most part on borrowed money, his various ventures into business of one kind or another were bringing him at least some small rewards. But his financial position was still very precarious. His debts were large and some of his creditors were impatient.

Some success he may have had but it was a far cry to Moscow and the overthrow of the Bolsheviks and he received a severe jolt when an old friend of his, Maria Schovalovsky, was lured back to Russia and never heard of again. She had defected from the Soviet Embassy in Paris and it had been Reilly who had helped her escape in a packing case. With her hair cut short and disguised as a man she had eventually reached America. As a reprisal, the Russians had arrested her father, but it was not long before she received letters from him begging her to return to assist in an escape plan he had. The letters seemed absolutely genuine but in reality were the work of G.P.U. forgers; their manufactured documents and letters were works of art and had lured countless victims back to Russia to face torture and death at the hands of Adamson, the secret police's Latvian chief executioner, and his assistants.

Adamson, who was the epitome of all that was base in human nature, had the unpleasant habit of taking his female victims from the J.O.K.* and raping them immediately prior to execution. He was almost as vicious as 'mad Dora', the Cheka female executioner, who, in a fit of blood lust, personally shot 700 prisoners in the space of a few nights before putting the hangman's noose round her own neck. After her mass murder, the prison cellars were filled with corpses. Torn off fingers and other parts of the human body scattered on the ground bore silent witness to hideous tortures.

Some women prisoners were shot when eight months' pregnant or two or three days after childbirth. Victims of the G.P.U., both male and female, when condemned to death, were usually taken from their cells with their hands tied, their noses stopped and their mouths gagged. At the scene of execution their hands were untied, they were told to walk through a

* The solitary confinement wing for women prisoners.

door and were shot in the back of the head. In the basement of the G.P.U.'s 'Inner Prison' in the Loubianka where countless executions took place, every stone was stained with blood and tears. Large groups were shot by the G.P.U. Special Service Regiment.

We must now return to 'The Trust' and its activities, on which much would depend in the event of a counter-revolutionary coup. Reilly's views were as follows: basically he had been impressed by what he had seen and heard of 'The Trust' but he was uncertain of the exact status in Russia of its leaders and the extent to which it might or might not have been infiltrated by Dzerjinsky's agents. From his various discussions with Boyce, Reilly knew that Boyce and the British Secret Service had some doubts about 'The Trust'.

Most of the traffic of spies into and out of Russia was through the Baltic states. Here and in Scandinavia, principally in Finland, the anti-Reds, very often in the guise of Bolsheviks, lived a strange existence devoted to conspiracy, the planning of escapes and the preparation of forged papers. Here, too, G.P.U. agents arrived from Russia pretending to be White Russians. Intrigue of every kind prevailed. At Reval, Boyce, at the head of his team of agents, kept watch on behalf of the British Secret Service. On the Russian side of the Baltic frontiers Michael Vladimiroff, one of Dzerjinsky's section chiefs, was ready to pounce. In the Baltic states, people who had arrived mysteriously from Russia disappeared just as mysteriously. They were for the most part pawns in the game and of little importance to either side. Often it was a case of a White Russian seeking private vengeance on another White

Russian. Sometimes the G.P.U. would liquidate one of its own agents in error.

Reilly, amid all his other activities in America, still maintained regular communication with the various counter-revolutionary groups outside Russia, who since Savinkoff's return to Moscow, were quarrelling among themselves more than ever. He also kept in touch with Boyce.

From the reports reaching Boyce from his spies, it seemed clear that the power of 'The Trust' was growing and that the movement included members of the Soviet Government itself. He was particularly impressed by the reports of two anti-Red agents who were acting as couriers between General Kutyepoff and 'The Trust'. These were Maria Schultz and her husband George Nicolaievich Radkevich. Although he was later to die a hero's death throwing a bomb in the G.P.U. offices in Moscow, George definitely played second fiddle to his wife. Both in her courage and in her hatred of Communism, Maria Vladimirovna Schultz was second only to Reilly himself. Slight of build and of plain but honest appearance, Maria Schultz had served four years of war as a private in the Russian army. A general's daughter whose family had been wiped out by the Bolsheviks, she had been one of the first to join the White Russian resistance movement. She was one of Kutyepoff's most trusted agents and, through 'The Window', had run the Red gauntlet in and out of Russia many times. Boyce had no doubts about her integrity.

Maria Schultz and other agents in touch with 'The Trust' urged the need for funds and assistance from outside Russia. Although this was nothing new, to Boyce it appeared not only that the movement was considerably stronger than the year before but also that the moment to strike at Bolshevism might well be near, in view of the growing differences between the Trotskyites and Stalin's supporters over the succession to Lenin, who had died in 1924.

In January, 1925, Boyce therefore wrote a long letter in code to Reilly explaining the importance of 'The Trust' and recommending him to meet the Schultzes in Paris. He wrote:

> I am introducing this scheme to you thinking it might perhaps replace the other big scheme you were working on but which fell through in such a disastrous manner. Incidentally, you would help me considerably by taking the matter up. The only thing I ask is that you keep our connection with this business from the knowledge of my department as, being a Government official, I am not supposed to be connected with any such enterprise. I know your interest in such a business where patience and perseverance against all sorts of intrigues and opposition are required and I know also you will look after my interests without my having to make some special agreement with you.

This was the first of a number of letters written in code or with invisible inks which passed between Boyce and Reilly in the first half of 1925 and which culminated in Reilly going to Paris in September to meet Boyce, General Kutyepoff and other leading counter-revolutionaries.

Cumming* had by now been replaced as Chief of the

* Cumming died in June, 1923.

S.I.S. and it is significant that in all the preliminary communications prior to Reilly's departure from America, there were none between Reilly and S.I.S. headquarters in London – only with Boyce. Boyce, in the letters he sent Reilly in the early months of 1925, while urging the master spy to co-operate with 'The Trust', made it quite clear that neither the British Government nor the British Secret Service, including Boyce himself, wished to be involved if anything went wrong. True to all Secret Service traditions, Reilly would be out on his own.

Reilly, for his part, was exhilarated by the news from Boyce. He suggested that 'The Trust's' representatives should come to America where Henry Ford could be approached for finance. He recommended to Boyce that the co-operation of Winston Churchill be sought to canvass the political support of anti-Communist governments throughout the world. To Boyce, he wrote:

> As regards a closer understanding with the international market, I think that to start with only one man is really important, and that is the irrepressible Marlborough.* I have always remained on good terms with him . . . His ear would always be open to something really sound, especially if it emanated from the minority interests.† He said as much in one of his very private and confidential letters to me.

Although eager to get to grips with the Bolsheviks, Reilly was nevertheless wary. Maria Schultz herself did

---

* 'Marlborough' was the code name for Churchill.
† 'Minority interests' denoted the anti-Communists.

not know the identity of 'The Trust' leaders and, for the time being, her immediate superiors would disclose neither to Boyce nor to anyone else the names of the top men. Reilly recognized the futility of trying to weld into one movement which might co-operate with 'The Trust' all the anti-Bolsheviks outside Russia, consisting as they did of monarchists, bourgeois and Social-Revolutionary elements, to say nothing of the various military cliques.

Reilly insisted to Boyce that 'The Trust' should first be persuaded to seek 'understandings' with the leaders of foreign powers, before launching a counter-revolution. 'Without such an understanding, arrived at very carefully and with great discretion in advance, the eventual re-organization cannot possibly rest on a solid base, especially from a financial point of view. In these two respects all the present manufacturers* put together cannot be of any help.'

'The Trust' leaders had no wish to send agents as far afield as America but were extremely keen to have Reilly's help and advice. Boyce therefore asked Reilly to communicate directly with one of 'The Trust's' more important agents in Helsinki, Nicolai Nicolaivich Bunakoff. Bunakoff would answer any questions Reilly wanted to ask provided he also sent Bunakoff 'another letter which he can show to the Moscow Centre or its representatives to the effect that you are interested in the commercial proposition submitted and putting forward any suggestion you may have to make and at the same time if possible give them something which will show that you are in a position to help them'.

The communications from Bunakoff were altogether

* Code word for 'counter-revolutionaries'.

too vague and, as he indicated in a letter to Boyce in March, Reilly was well aware that the patience of non-Russian supporters of a counter-revolution was nearly exhausted after seven years of waiting. Despite Boyce's continuing encouraging news about the strength of 'The Trust' movement, Reilly might have hesitated to involve himself too deeply had it not been for the state of his personal finances. However, since his boyhood he had been a confirmed gambler. He wrote to Boyce:

Much as I am concerned about my own personal affairs which, as you know, are in a hellish state, I am at any moment, if I see the right people and prospects of real action, prepared to chuck everything else and devote myself entirely to the Syndicate's interests.

I was fifty-one yesterday and I want to do something worthwhile, whilst I can. All the rest does not matter. I am quite sure that you, although younger, feel likewise.

Needless to say how deeply grateful I am to you for bringing me into this situation. I feel sure that if we are dealing with the right people, we will be able to work out something not only of the greatest interest generally, but possibly also of the greatest advantage to ourselves.

I shall write to you some more later.

Meantime –

Yours ever,-

On April 4th, Reilly received from Helsinki a copy of a letter which the leaders of 'The Trust' had sent Bunakoff in which they had suggested that the simplest and quickest solution was for Reilly to visit Russia, meet 'The Trust's' executive and judge its strength for himself.

On receipt of the letter from Bunakoff, he immediately wrote to Boyce:

> I am not only willing but anxious to do so and am prepared to come out as soon as I have arranged my affairs here. Of course, I would undertake this tour of inspection only after very thorough consultation with you and Engineer B.* Whilst there is no limit to which I am not prepared to go in order to help putting this new process on the market, I would naturally hate to provide a Roman holiday for the competitors. I think that I am not exaggerating in presuming that a successful inspection of the factory† by me and the presentation of a fully substantiated technical report would produce a considerable impression in the interested quarters and generally facilitate to realization of the scheme.

Two months later, Boyce had made arrangements for a preliminary meeting between Reilly and representatives of 'The Trust' but Reilly delayed once again, giving business as an excuse. The excuse was genuine: Reilly was desperately trying to stave off his creditors and to restore his private affairs to some sort of order. His efforts were not successful. He decided to return to Europe.

On September 3rd, Reilly reached Paris accompanied by the ever loving Pepita. Boyce met him on arrival.

In Paris, Reilly had lengthy discussions with Boyce,

---

* Bunakoff.
† 'The Trust' leaders.

General Kutyepoff, Burtzoff – former head of the Social-Revolutionaries' Secret Service – and his old friend Grammatikoff. It was decided that the only way to establish whether co-operation with 'The Trust' might lead to a genuine counter-revolution was for Reilly to meet 'The Trust' leaders either in Helsinki or near the Russo–Finnish frontier. If necessary, Reilly was ready to risk a journey into Russia itself.

A few days later, Reilly set out for Helsinki which he reached on September 21st. On the way, he stopped in Berlin, where he saw Vladimir Orloff, Grammatikoff's old friend and his one-time helper in the Zinoviev Letter affair. Orloff spoke with respect of 'The Trust's' powers. In Helsinki, for the first time, Reilly met Bunakoff, Maria Schultz, her husband, and Boyce's second-in-command who was as enthusiastic as his superior about the potentialities of 'The Trust'. Reilly was as impressed as everyone else had been with Maria Schultz and was encouraged by her reports of the situation inside Russia. From Helsinki he wrote:

If only twenty-five per cent of what she said is based on facts (and not on self-induced delusion, as is so often the case when the wish is father of the will) then there is really something entirely new, powerful and worth-while going on in Russia.

'The Trust's' leaders had failed to turn up as expected but shortly after Reilly's arrival in Helsinki, Bunakoff received a message from Russia that Reilly should proceed to Wyborg, close to the Russian frontier. There, the leaders would await him on September 24th.

Reilly, Bunakoff and the two Schultzes proceeded immediately to Wyborg where they met Alexander

Alexandrovich Yakushev and two other members of 'The Trust'. Yakushev claimed to hold a senior position in the G.P.U. and Reilly knew that, since 1921, Yakushev had also been acting as a spy for Boyce, feeding him with intelligence reports on Russia. He cross-examined Yakushev very closely and at length. He seemed satisfied that Yakushev was not an agent-provocateur and that 'The Trust' was indeed a powerful anti-Soviet underground movement.

Yakushev urged Reilly to visit Moscow for two or three days to meet what was in effect the secret 'Shadow Cabinet' of the future Russian Government. By meeting all the leaders of 'The Trust', he could assure himself of the importance of the movement. 'The Trust' had so many people in high places that there was no risk to Reilly in crossing the border. On the other hand, it was difficult for 'The Trust' leaders themselves to leave Russia for a conference: most were in such senior positions within the Soviet State that their absence would be conspicuous. Yakushev said that he himself would have to return to Russia at once.

Reilly agreed to leave the next day for Moscow with a passport which Yakushev provided in the name of Nicolas Nicolaivich Steinberg. The die was cast. Yakushev departed at once for Russia, leaving his two colleagues from 'The Trust' to escort Reilly across the border.

It is very doubtful whether Reilly believed the risk to be as small as Yakushev asserted. The previous year, he had confided to Sir Paul Dukes his intention of returning to Russia 'to fight', but before leaving New York and with his own finances in a desperate state, he had yet made certain provisions for Pepita in the event of his death. Two days before he met Yakushev and before he knew that he would definitely be invited to Moscow, Reilly had written Pepita:

> Above all, don't worry about me. I feel perfectly well and my heart is overflowing with love for you. You are never out of my thoughts.
>
> We love each other so completely that it is impossible that such love should not reap its full reward both in spiritual and material happiness.

It was the letter of a man who had not only made his decision but was also aware of the possibility that he might never return.

To Reilly, whatever the risks might be, the opportunity was one he could not miss. If 'The Trust' was as powerful as it seemed, it only needed support from outside Russia to topple the Bolshevik régime. 'The Trust's' leaders looked to him for advice and guidance. If he failed them, he would be failing the millions of Russians who were living under the Red Terror. Above all, it was the best chance yet to redeem his failure of 1918 – the chance for which he had waited seven long years. His personal affairs were in such a mess that he had little to lose except his life and this he was not afraid to do. In any case, if the worst happened and he were captured, the powers of 'The Trust' might save him from execution just as they had saved Savinkoff.

Reilly wrote a farewell letter to Pepita, which he gave to Bunakoff to forward to her only if he failed to return. Setting off to face the unknown, he secretly crossed the Russian frontier on September 25th in the company of the two Russians from 'The Trust' and George Radkevich, Maria Schultz's husband. Radkevich went only a short distance into Russia and then returned to Finland, to report that Reilly and his companions had safely boarded a train for Leningrad.*

The twentieth-century Napoleon was returning from exile. The one-time plague of the German General Staff and the man whom the Bolsheviks had most cause to fear, was back in Russia to gather new battalions around him.

Boyce received a postcard from Reilly dated September 27th indicating all was well. The postmark was Moscow.

It was the last that Boyce or anyone else heard from Reilly and an announcement in *Izvestia* a few days later seemed to set the seal on Reilly's fate. The announcement was brief but to the point: 'On the night of September 28th/29th four smugglers attempted to cross the Finnish frontier. Two were killed, one, a Finnish soldier, taken prisoner and the fourth, mortally wounded, died on the way to Leningrad.'

It was the night on which Reilly was due back in Finland. Finnish soldiers had heard the shooting and a White Russian sympathizer in the Finnish frontier police who was to escort Reilly back across the border had failed to return. Intelligence agents received reports that Russian soldiers across the frontier had been seen carrying away bodies. The mortally wounded man who had died on the train to Leningrad was said to be Reilly.

The heart of the valiant lone warrior beat no more. A dramatic life in a dramatic age was over.

But was it?

* The name of Petrograd was changed to Leningrad in 1924.

Part Three

XI

Most choice, forsaken.

KING LEAR

In the months that followed Reilly's disappearance into Russia, neither Boyce nor his agents nor those of General Kutyepoff could obtain any confirmation of Reilly's death or otherwise. Every enquiry ran up against a brick wall.

Maria Schultz, who obviously feared the worst, made several visits to Russia and repeatedly pressed Edward Opperput, her main contact in 'The Trust', to find out exactly what had happened. Opperput, who held a senior position in 'The Trust', could not or would not say anything.

Pepita Reilly was desperately anxious to learn the truth. If the Russians had killed or captured her husband, she thought that they would surely have publicized their victory over Russia's greatest enemy. The silence seemed to prove that Reilly was still alive.

Pepita telephoned Thwaites and tried in vain to obtain Boyce's help. At the crucial time of Reilly's entry into Russia, Boyce had been in London – conveniently absent from the scene of operations. His assistant had been in charge in Reval but even he had not questioned Reilly about his vital meeting with Yakushev.

From Helsinki and Stockholm, Boyce now sent consoling but not very helpful letters to Pepita. Four weeks after Reilly's disappearance, when it was clear that something had gone seriously wrong, the British Secret Service was hurriedly extricating itself from a situation which was politically explosive. Although in the past it had been eager to use Reilly's talents, the S.I.S. was now anxious to disclaim all connection with him. Boyce, on instructions from above, failed to keep an appointment with Pepita in Paris. Instead he wrote to her from London as follows:

I have had no later information and do not now see how I can get any as my only possible source, I hear, has left Helsinki and is now on his way to Paris to see you. You will therefore be advised earlier than I shall. I don't know when I shall hear any more about it as I find urgent business now which takes me abroad again immediately and prevents me coming to Paris.

Furthermore, I shall have no permanent address for some time, but will let you know later where I am to be found if you will give instructions for letters to be forwarded from your present address. *Au revoir* and trusting you will soon get more definite and satisfactory information.

The 'only possible source' was Bunakoff. He had no news but brought Reilly's farewell letter.

Pepita traced Boyce to Berners Hotel in London only to find that he had received instructions from his superiors that it would be dangerous for a Secret Service official to be seen in her company. He asked for all Reilly's private papers including letters which

Boyce himself had written him. They would be of the utmost value to the Bolsheviks, he said, if they were to fall into Soviet hands.

Stephen Alley and George Hill did their best to find out the truth about Reilly's disappearance and Hill went to see both Don Gregory at the Foreign Office and Sir Archibald Sinclair,* M.P., the former secretary of Winston Churchill. Gregory, then an Assistant Under-Secretary of State, and Sinclair were both personal friends of Reilly but Hill found himself powerless. Gregory wished to dissociate the Foreign Office from the whole affair and Sinclair said the matter was too dangerous to discuss. The absence of information or the deliberate silence, whichever it might be, was complete.

Although the S.I.S. tried to exert pressure on Pepita to maintain silence about Reilly's presumed death, she inserted a brief notice in the 'Deaths' column of *The Times* on December 15th, 1925, in the hope that officialdom could be prodded into revealing something. It read:

Reilly – On the 28th Sept., killed near the village of Allekull, Russia by G.P.U. troops, Captain Sidney George Reilly, M.C., late R.A.F., beloved husband of Pepita N. Reilly.

---

* Sir Archibald Sinclair hinted that the Government might pay compensation to Pepita for Reilly's death. In the event, she received nothing. And such payment would have been tantamount to an official admission that Reilly was engaged on a mission for the Secret Intelligence Service. Furthermore, Pepita was not Reilly's wife in law. When Pepita complained that Cumming had knowingly connived at her bigamous marriage and had done nothing to prevent it, she was blackmailed into silence with the threat that her British passport would be taken from her if she did not keep quiet about this.

In the course of the next few days the British press devoted column after column to accounts of Reilly's amazing exploits. According to one correspondent, he had even disguised himself as Lenin and carried out an inspection of the Red army. A great many of these stories were either totally untrue or grossly inaccurate. Despite this flurry in the press,* the rulers in the Kremlin maintained their enigmatic silence and in spite of questions in the House of Commons the Foreign Office was as uncommunicative as ever.

The Foreign Office, although admitting that Reilly was known to them, said they were unable to make any official statement. They could not state whether or not Reilly was engaged in Foreign Office work.

Not only Britain but France, too, mourned the presumed death of the master spy. In December, 1924, Reilly had provided both the British and the French Governments with details of a Communist rising planned to take place in Paris and northern France. At first M. Herriot, the French Premier, had ignored them but Baldwin's Government provided the French with conclusive proof and the Red ringleaders were rounded up and expelled from France.† 'Let France remember with gratitude,' wrote *La Liberté*, 'this loyal servant of the Intelligence Service.'

As the months passed, the opinion of General Kutyepoff and of many of his associates hardened into

---

* *The Times*, presumably as a result of official pressure, was the only newspaper to make no editorial comment. Harold Williams of *The Times* wrote to Pepita that Reilly 'died well and in the best of causes' but stated that if *The Times* had published no comment this was because of 'certain political complications'.

† It is not clear whether René Marchand, the man who had betrayed Reilly in 1918, was involved in this plot.

a belief that Reilly had been lured back to Russia by agents-provocateurs and that he was indeed dead. There were suspicions that 'The Trust' was a Bolshevik plot and British Secret Service agents who had assisted or encouraged Reilly in his mission were either relieved of their duties or given new assignments. Boyce, who had been dealing with Yakushev for the past five years, was 'found' a job by Alley with the Société Francaise de Tabacs in Paris. M.I.1C. feared that it had been thoroughly fooled by the Bolsheviks. Rather than admit that they had been hoodwinked, those in 'informed circles' began to circulate a rumour that Reilly – of all people – might have defected to the Reds.

Towards the end of 1926, General von Monkewitz, Kutyepoff's right-hand man, vanished. It was believed that he too had either been lured to destruction or had for some time been an agent of the Bolsheviks. Nevertheless, Maria Schultz, Kutyepoff's chief spy, who was in closest contact with 'The Trust' through Opperput, had personally seen a mass of evidence indicating the strength of anti-Bolshevik feeling in 'The Trust'. She had seen for herself the anti-Bolshevik propaganda printed and distributed by 'The Trust' in Russia, had attended secret meetings at which 'The Trust' leaders had harangued their members with violent tirades against the Kremlin 'murderers'. Perhaps 'The Trust' had been infiltrated at its perimeter by a few G.P.U. agents, but of the integrity of the majority, Maria Schultz was convinced. She had tremendous faith in Opperput, 'The Trust's' 'Shadow Minister for Finance' and felt certain that Reilly was still alive, even if 'The Trust' could not confide in her.

Then in April, 1927, the truth came out. Opperput arrived in Finland to confess that all along he had been a member of the G.P.U. counter-espionage. A tall red-headed man with a small beard, Opperput had served as an officer in the Tsar's army. His duplicity knew no bounds and Kutyepoff and Maria Schultz were appalled to learn from him that 'The Trust' was indeed nothing but a vast Bolshevik plot to uncover anti-Reds both inside and outside Russia and to lure their leaders, and Reilly in particular, into the hands of the G.P.U. 'The Trust' was riddled with agents-provocateurs; Yakushev, his deputy, General Potapoff, and all 'The Trust's' leaders were in fact the *élite* of the G.P.U.'s agents. 'The Trust' was the brain-child of the diabolical Artuzoff, the chief of the K.R.O., the G.P.U.'s counter-intelligence department.

To give 'The Trust' the appearance of authenticity, the G.P.U. had deliberately fomented anti-Bolshevism throughout Russia, printing and distributing anti-Soviet literature and organizing genuine counter-revolutionary unrest. However, the leaders had always had the situation under control and could pounce whenever they chose. Now that 'The Trust's' main objective, the capture of Reilly, had been achieved and anti-Bolshevik suspicions outside Russia aroused, 'The Trust' would probably be disbanded or put into cold storage. And Menjinsky, who had succeeded Dzerjinsky* as chief of the G.P.U., would certainly liquidate even the best of his own agents once they had served their purpose. To save his life, Opperput had now defected.

* Dzerjinsky died in mysterious circumstances in 1926. His successor Menjinsky, was said to have had a persecution complex. A lawyer from a well-to-do family, he had nothing but contempt for the working class which he called 'a stupidity discovered by the intelligentsia'. Essentially an opportunist, the only real streak of 'Red' in him was on his finger-nails and toe-nails which he dyed with henna.

According to Opperput, Reilly had indeed reached Moscow safely and, still unsuspecting, had had a number of discussions with Yakushev, Artuzoff himself and his right-hand man, Styrne. Opperput had been present at these discussions. At first, it had not been the G.P.U.'s intention to kill Reilly. If they did so, anti-Bolsheviks outside Russia would have guessed the true nature of 'The Trust' and, in consequence, 'The Trust' would have had to be disbanded and a major source of intelligence about anti-Bolshevik activities would have been lost. The G.P.U. plan had been to let Reilly return to Finland as a proof to the outside world of the power of 'The Trust' and so that he might lull Kutyepoff and other counter-revolutionaries into inaction. Reilly could have spread the story that 'The Trust' was powerful enough to move on its own and that counter-revolutionary agitations outside Russia should cease lest they compromise 'The Trust'.

Once Reilly had reached Russia, the views of some of the G.P.U. chiefs changed. Bolshevism's greatest enemy was at their mercy; it would be madness to let him go. A considerable argument developed within the hierarchy of the Secret Police and opinions were equally divided on the matter. In the end, the question of Reilly's fate was referred to the Politbureau. It was Stalin himself who ruled that Reilly could not be allowed to leave Russia alive.

Opperput stated that after two days in Moscow, during which his fate was so hotly debated, Reilly was quietly arrested and placed in the Butyrsky prison. A faked shooting incident on the Finnish border was staged by the G.P.U. to deceive the world into believing that Reilly had been shot in mistake for a smuggler.

Reilly, said Opperput, had been well treated in

prison for some time, allowed to go for drives and given his favourite brand of whisky. His persistent refusal to talk, however, could have had only one consequence. No-one could long resist the interrogation methods of the G.P.U. and eventually, like many before him, Reilly had broken down. When the G.P.U. had extracted from him what they could, he was shot.

Opperput's account of Reilly's fate had all the semblance of truth but there was more than a possibility that Opperput's whole story was a tissue of lies and yet another tactical move on the part of the G.P.U. Might not the G.P.U. be worried because 'The Trust' organization was now suspect, and might it not have sent just such a man as Opperput with just such a story to convince the counter-revolutionaries that he at least could be trusted? Might not Opperput be the spearhead of a new G.P.U. plot?

The possibility that Opperput's flight to Finland was a double-cross increased when he escorted Maria Schultz, who was determined to find out the truth, back into Russia. Opperput returned safely to Finland but Maria Schultz was never to be heard of again.

Further, even if part of Opperput's story was true, he could only have obtained at second-hand the details of Reilly's imprisonment and death. There was a small but significant error in Opperput's story: Reilly never touched whisky.

Soon after Opperput's 'defection', the Russians announced the discovery of an anti-Soviet plot directed by General Kutyepoff.* There were mass executions

---

* Kutyepoff, a monarchist who could never come to terms with the Social-Revolutionary Savinkoff, was himself to be sensationally kidnapped in broad daylight by G.P.U. agents in a Paris street three years later.

throughout Russia.

Finally, in June, 1927, the Russians, in an official communiqué, and nearly two years after his disappearance, made a reference to Reilly. Voikoff, the Russian Minister in Warsaw, had been assassinated. The Russians claimed this was the work of British secret agents. An official communiqué from Moscow, dated June 8th, stated:

In connection with this criminal murder which followed a whole series of direct and indirect attacks on the part of the British Government on U.S.S.R. institutions abroad, and the rupture by Great Britain of diplomatic relations with the U.S.S.R., the Soviet Government deems it necessary at the present moment to make public a series of other facts sufficiently characteristic of the British Government and its varied organizations in U.S.S.R. territory.

In the summer of 1925, a certain merchant carrying a Soviet passport with the name of Steinberg was wounded and arrested by the Frontier Guard while illegally crossing the Finnish frontier.

During the inquiry a witness declared that his name was actually Sidney George Riley, and that he was an English spy, a captain of the Royal Air Force, one of the chief organizers of 'Lockhart's plot', who by sentence of the Tribunal of December 3rd, 1918, had been declared an outlaw.

Riley declared that he came to Russia for the special purpose of organizing terroristic acts, arson and revolts, and that when coming from America he had seen Mr. Churchill, Chancellor of the Exchequer, who personally instructed him as to the reorganization of terroristic and other acts calculated to create a diversion.

His written testimony is in the possession of the Government. Riley's evidence was entirely corroborated by material seized during further arrests.*

There was no word of Reilly's ultimate fate, his name was spelt incorrectly and the story of the frontier incident was different both from the original story put out by the G.P.U. that Reilly had been mortally wounded and also from Opperput's version.

Three months after this communiqué, in September, 1927, *Izvestia* published some rather innocuous correspondence which was purported to have passed between Reilly and 'an ex-Russian officer called Bunakoff' in which Reilly was accused of writing: 'the only possibility of combating Bolshevism is to organize attacks on the commissars'. If this was the most damning evidence the Russians could produce of Reilly's anti-Red activities their case was not a strong one.

In the same month, reports appeared in the Russian press of the trial of five Russian terrorists accused of throwing bombs in the Communist Club at Leningrad in June, 1927. The reports were very curious. Katanyan, Attorney-General for the G.P.U. and Assistant Prosecutor of the Supreme Court, stated that the five terrorists had been 'in close contact with the Secret Intelligence Service of England'. The Moscow press went on to say: 'On Sunday last, the G.P.U. announced the forthcoming trial of six more alleged British spies.' Reilly was mentioned as 'the British chief directing terrorist

* By an extraordinary coincidence, the expulsion of Trotsky and Zinoviev from the Communist Party was announced on the same day!

acts in Soviet Russia', and as 'a confidential agent of Churchill'.

If the Russians had executed Reilly in 1925, he could hardly be directing terrorism in 1927. Or was he? Had the Russians let him slip through their fingers? After first maintaining complete silence for two years, and then eventually stating that they had captured Reilly, why did they not expose all the 'machinations' of this spy of the 'evil Churchill' and the iniquitous British Secret Service? Could the master-minds who had devised 'The Trust' have failed to see the propaganda possibilities?

The situation was further confused by a report from a White Russian who escaped from a Soviet prison and found his way across Siberia to Tientsin in October, 1927. He stated that Reilly was still alive in the prison at Orel but insane.

In 1927, the question of Reilly's activities was raised in the House of Commons by Mr. Saklatvala, a Communist M.P. Mr. Locker-Lampson, then Parliamentary Under-Secretary of State for Foreign Affairs, denied that Reilly had worked for Bruce Lockhart in 1918 and that Reilly had tried to enter the Soviet Union with Foreign Office knowledge in 1925, adding: 'I have no information regarding Mr. Reilly's alleged entry into Russia in 1925 beyond what has already appeared in the press.'

Officially, of course, the Foreign Office never has any dealings with Secret Service agents and it would be astonishing for any Government to admit to the activities of any of its secret agents.

In November, a report which reached Riga from Moscow also stated that Reilly was still alive. It was said that he had been tortured and that his 'confessions' had led to the arrests of a number of spies by the G.P.U.

G.P.U. tortures were crude but effective. They consisted usually of tying the victim in a strait-jacket to an iron bunk. The strait-jacket was his only clothing; he had no blanket, no food and was unable to go to the lavatory. With a gag in his mouth and a stopper in his rectum he would be given periodic beatings with rubber poles. There were many suicides; some prisoners preferred to set fire to their mattresses and burn themselves to death rather than face the G.P.U. thugs. At the time of Reilly's disappearance, the number of executions carried out by the G.P.U. and its predecessor, the Cheka, was said to exceed 250,000. Excluding countless thousands condemned to the rigours of Siberia, it was estimated that some 1,300,000 people were incarcerated in Russia's six thousand odd gaols.

No doubt, if the G.P.U. had wanted to, it would have devised even more vicious treatment for so important a prisoner as Reilly. Dukis, the commandant of the 'Inner Prison', was noted for his sadism.

In London, there were two aching hearts, those of Pepita and Caryll Houselander. Neither woman was ever sure what had happened to the man in their lives. Caryll, who continued to love the man who had deserted her for Pepita, told friends of another mystical experience which occurred ten years after Reilly's disappearance. She spoke of having 'travelled far', of having been in a prison cell with 'someone' and of sharing his sufferings. Almost certainly she was referring to Reilly and, if there was any substance to her vision, Reilly must have been alive in 1935 on the occasion of this experience.

After the several contradictory statements in the

Russian press in 1927, which only added to the confusion, Moscow reverted to its enigmatic silence.

There were many rumours to the effect that Reilly was still alive, or was dead, or had escaped from first one prison then another. The silence of the Soviet Government led some people in M.I.5, the British Counter-Intelligence Service, to suspect that Reilly had made a deal with the Bolsheviks. Perhaps he had sold out to them because there was no prospect of settling his debts. The Russians would obviously disclose little or nothing if Reilly was now working for them. He was, after all, a Russian by birth and many people had changed sides more than once since the Russian Revolution. There were rumours that he was working in China as an agent of the Soviet Government.

There was also the possibility that Reilly had faked his own death at the Finnish frontier just as he had staged a 'suicide' in his youth at Odessa. He might have realized that 'The Trust' was not genuine and that all his years of struggling against the Bolsheviks had been in vain and so vanished to assume a new identity – perhaps in South America again. This theory would also account for the initial silence of the Russians. Later, when the G.P.U. were satisfied that the British knew as little as they did about Reilly's whereabouts they issued a deliberately vague propaganda story that they had captured Reilly and that he had 'confessed'. The G.P.U.'s intention might have been to ensure that if Reilly did turn up in Britain again, whatever story he told would be disbelieved by the British Intelligence Services. He would be permanently discredited. This theory may sound implausible but Dzerjinsky, who was still alive at the time, was quite capable of producing a scheme as devious as this.

When, in 1931, the *Evening Standard* published a melodramatic serial on Reilly's Russian adventures under the signature of Pepita Reilly, 'Sidney Reilly's wife', there were renewed demands in the House of Commons for the Foreign Office to press the Soviet Government for news of Reilly's fate. One result of the *Evening Standard* serial was to bring Margaret out of hiding in Brussels. Legally she was the only Mrs. Reilly and the newspaper was compelled to pay her several thousand pounds in damages! Elkin, Mathews and Marrot, publishers of the story in book form, also found themselves paying damages to Margaret and the book was withdrawn from sale after only 2,000 copies had been printed. The *Evening Standard* and the publishers both settled out of court and the public never learnt of Reilly's excursions into bigamy.

At the same time, Pepita's flat in Paris was burgled several times – presumably by G.P.U. agents – and some of Reilly's papers, including a file marked 'Zinoviev', were stolen.

By now, reports had been reaching British Intelligence Services that Reilly had himself appeared in various parts of the world. Reports that he was still alive in Russia, in America, in the Middle East and elsewhere continued up to the end of the Second World War.

Among other reports which came out of Russia was one from a Polish official called Brunovsky who had been in the Butyrsky Prison, but who had been eventually released. A prison friend of his had learnt that an important British spy was in the prison. Brunovsky, who was more interested in his own release than in British spies and who had never heard of Reilly, made a brief note of a message from his prison friend. The message was: 'British Officer Reilly. Persia. Father-in-Law.' On being set free, Brunovsky was bewildered by this message written in Russian on a piece of linen which he had sewn into the lining of his coat. Whether the message originated from Reilly himself or from another captured spy in the pay of the British S.I.S. is not known. What is certain is that very few people knew of Reilly's old association with Persia and that *testi*, the Russian word for 'Father-in-Law', might well have been Le S.T.1 – and S.T.1 was Reilly's code name in M.I.1C.

This curious message might have meant that Reilly was either planning to escape to Persia or had in fact escaped to Persia.

There was a remarkable sequel to this report a few years later. In 1931, a British official in the Middle East reported that he had been visiting a Russian tramp steamer when he had been approached by a Russian sailor who told him in perfect English that he had to desert from the ship at all costs. The British official arranged for the sailor to come to his bungalow near the port. The sailor claimed that he was Reilly and that he had escaped from Odessa. He said that he had been held prisoner in Moscow for a long time but had recently been moved under a guard of five police officers to Odessa for further questioning. He had succeeded in getting a revolver from one of the guards and had shot his way to freedom. Now, having escaped from Russia as a sailor on board ship he needed money and clothing. The British official provided both and a bed for the night. In the morning, the man who said he was Reilly had gone. It is not difficult to disappear in the Middle East.

When Geoffrey Shakespeare, Liberal M.P. for Norwich asked the British Government in June, 1931, if it had any news of Reilly, he was told succinctly: 'No further information can be obtained.'

George Hill spent the Second World War in Moscow as liaison officer with the N.K.V.D.* He learnt nothing from the Russians about Reilly, yet in 1945, at the end of the war, an N.K.V.D. man did tell another member of the British Mission that Reilly was still alive, in prison but insane.

In 1956, an approach was made direct to Khrushchev and Bulganin for information about Reilly, but none was forthcoming.

---

* Narodny Kommissariat Knutrennyich Del. The new name given by Stalin in 1934 to the G.P.U.

Part Four

XII

Ask you what provocation I had?

POPE

In March, 1966, reports in the British press that the author was in possession of certain new information about Sidney Reilly and intended to publish a book about him produced an immediate reaction from Moscow. Within days, *Nedelya*, the Sunday magazine edition of *Izvestia*, published an article of some length claiming that the Cheka was fully aware of the notorious 'Lockhart Plot' of 1918 and of Reilly's part in it from its very inception. Photographs of a Cheka agent-provocateur, and of a special pass which Bruce Lockhart had given him accompanied the article. But, as a leading article in *The Times* was quick to point out, the author's father had made it clear in his book *Memoirs of a British Agent* that he was aware all the time that the man concerned was probably an agent-provocateur.

A translation of the *Nedelya* article is as follows:

CHEKISTS – ON THE SUBJECT OF THEIR WORK

Under the Name of Schmidhen

Only 48 years afterwards, has it become possible to name the person who played the leading part in liquidating Lockhart's counter-revolutionary plot. This page tells how Chekists managed to track down the conspirators.

Worn pages, numerous underlinings and markings in the margins silently bear witness to the fact that countless people have held in their hands the many volumes that have been published on the Lockhart affair. It would appear that all there is to know has been told and that there is nothing new to disclose. Take, for instance, a document headed by the commonplace word 'Petition'. Its authors – fifteen lawyers, defending in court the participants in the plot of K. Kalamatiano and A. Friede,* who were condemned to death – appealed to the Presidium of Cheka for a reduced sentence. Where the document sets out the grounds of appeal, the lawyers mention the name 'Schmidhen' as a collaborator of Lockhart's who, for some reason, was not brought to trial.

Indeed, it seems strange that this participant in the plot escaped punishment. Schmidhen is a well-known figure. In archives and in historical literature he is always mentioned as one of Lockhart's collaborators. His fate is not generally known even if, initially, it appeared that he did not deserve to be remembered. Yet the document which lies before us awakens interest in this man. Why was this conspirator never in the dock?

---

* Colonel Friede served on the Russian General Staff. He was a fellow conspirator of Reilly and Kalamatiano, the head of the U.S. Secret Service in Russia. Peters, Vice-President of the Cheka in 1918, is on record as saying that of the various Allied Secret Services operating in Russia that of America was the most compromised in the 'Lockhart Plot'.

The final disclosures are a pleasant reward for some arduous research.

In 1918, to maintain the fight against the counter-revolution and to find out, in very confused circumstances, the direction from which the enemy's main efforts would come, F. E. Dzerjinsky entrusted to a small group of Chekists the task of infiltrating into one of the counter-revolutionary movements and of tracking down the organizers of the plot. Understandably, those assigned to this group assumed false names. One of them went under the surname 'Schmidhen'.

After Dzerjinsky's briefing, the group left for Petrograd, for although the Soviet Government was now in Moscow, the centre of counter-revolutionary activity still remained in the former capital. Posing as representatives of the Moscow counter-revolutionary underground movement who were trying to establish contact with their Petrograd counterparts, the Chekists had no difficulty in finding many 'like-minded' people in the turmoil of the revolution.

One day, while walking along the embankment of the river Neva, they stopped before a poster outside the Lettish Club (which was opposite the Admiralty). The poster announced that there would be a buffet-dance that evening. In that time of famine, a buffet was an unbelievable luxury in a club, and this attracted the attention of Schmidhen.

'Let's go into this centre of culture,' he suggested to his comrade, Sprogis.

That evening, Schmidhen and Sprogis appeared at the Lettish Club. These gay young officers, familiar with the ways of society, could mix easily with strangers. Young waitresses willingly chatted to the newcomers, telling them of the happy carefree time sailors could have in the club.

It was not difficult to find out that these evenings at the club occurred quite frequently and that the club's patrons were naval personnel from a guardship anchored nearby. Important people from the Admiralty also visited the club.

'And who provides the food for the buffet?' asked Schmidhen.

'The captain of the ship takes care of that. He also comes here himself,' confided the waitresses. They added: 'He is a serious man. He practically never dances and seems to prefer talking.'

The Chekists also learned a number of things which led them to suspect that someone was using these evenings as camouflage for other and more sinister activities.

On one occasion, a group of military men attracted their attention. Although they were accompanied by women, the latter kept somewhat apart from the men. As soon as the orchestra started up, the ladies left for the dance floor and the men began to converse among themselves.

One evening it was learnt that the captain of the guardship and his officers had arrived.

Schmidhen whispered to Sprogis:

'Invite the captain's lady to dance.'

The advice was naturally taken as an order and Sprogis whirled round with the lady in a gay polka.

This was sufficient to attract the attention of those in whom the Chekists were interested. It was not long before they made their acquaintance and it soon became clear that the Chekists had come into touch with the leaders of the counter-revolutionary organization, connected with the English Naval Attaché, Cromie, who was Lockhart's right-hand man.

Cromie used to stress that he had remained in Petrograd for a worthy purpose: to prevent the Russian Fleet from being seized by the Germans. In fact, his diplomatic passport was only a cover and he was trying hard to help the White Guard underground movement to consolidate its forces for the fight against Soviet rule.

Gradually, Schmidhen and his comrades gained the confidence of the conspirators. Two months later, the leaders of the counter-revolutionary organization said it would be useful if Schmidhen were introduced to the Naval Attaché of the British Embassy. That was indeed an achievement.

The first meeting between Cromie and Schmidhen and his comrades took place in an hotel, then called Frantsuskaia. The Chekists were presented as 'reliable people who could be trusted'. At the same time, Cromie introduced the Chekists to the experienced English spy, Sidney Reilly.

The English insisted that Schmidhen should leave immediately for Moscow to see Lockhart, Head of the Diplomatic Mission. Cromie gave him a sealed packet containing a letter of recommendation.

The Chekists spent the night before their departure at the Hotel Select and early in the morning there was an insistent knock on their door. On the threshold stood Sidney Reilly.

'Will there be any difficulty in handing over the letter to Lockhart? Do you need my assistance?' he asked with exaggerated politeness.

It was clear that such a surprise visit from an English agent had only one purpose: to verify that the letter had not been lost and had not fallen into other hands. After making sure that his fears were groundless, Reilly left the hotel in good spirits.

Schmidhen and Sprogis were aware of the possibility that they might be shadowed in Moscow. Therefore, on arriving in the capital, they walked from the station through small passages and side-streets in preference to the main thoroughfares.

The same day the letter was on Dzerjinsky's desk.

Next day, Schmidhen and Sprogis went to Lockhart's Moscow flat with Cromie's letter. In his book *Storm over Russia*,* which was published abroad in 1924, Lockhart wrote the following: 'I was dining, when the bell rang and my servant told me of the arrival of two people. One of them was a pale young man of small stature, who was called "Schmidhen" . . .

'Schmidhen brought me a letter from Cromie, which I carefully checked . . . but I ascertained that the letter was, without doubt, in Cromie's handwriting. The letter contained a reference to information that I had sent to Cromie with the help of the Swedish Consul General. Typical of such a brave officer as Cromie was the phrase that he was preparing to leave Russia and intended then to "bang the door behind him!" . . .'

Schmidhen pretended that he was a second lieutenant of the Tsarist Army and to be in touch with the influential commanding officers of the Lettish Rifles. According to him, several of these were disillusioned, had changed their attitude toward the Soviet authorities and were ready, at the first opportunity, to re-align themselves with the Allies. Naturally, in the eyes of Lockhart, Schmidhen was one of them.

Lockhart swallowed the bait. He was trying to stir up

* This refers to *Memoirs of a British Agent*, first published in 1932.

the Lettish troops, who guarded the Kremlin and other Government units, into action against the Soviet authorities. He then aimed to bring down the Soviet Government with the aid of counter-revolutionary officer cadres of the former Tsarist army. In Schmidhen, Lockhart saw first of all someone who could help him to find a reliable collaborator among the commanders of the Lettish regiments.

'Your main and foremost problem,' he instructed Schmidhen, 'is to arrest and kill Lenin – yes, yes, indeed, to kill him, because if Lenin manages to escape arrest, our enterprise will fail.'

Recommending Schmidhen to resort to bribery, Lockhart said that there was as much money as might be needed for the purpose.

Naturally, Lockhart was extremely careful. He did not disclose his whole plan at once but only after several meetings with Schmidhen. All the time he was checking up on his new acquaintances.

At one of these meetings, Schmidhen, following a plan approved by Dzerjinsky, recommended to Lockhart that he enter into direct contact with General Poole, who was in Archangel, and discuss with him arrangements for the defection of the Lettish Rifles, who were at the Archangel frontier, to the side of the Allies.

In order to influence Poole, the Cheka wanted Schmidhen to meet him personally, but trying to achieve a direct meeting between the Letts and Poole would have been risky, as it might have roused Lockhart's suspicions. But once again the Chekists were cunning. They were certain that Lockhart would not accept this proposal because he had no opportunity to establish direct communication with Poole. At the same time, they hoped that the proposal would interest him sufficiently to supply Schmidhen with a pass that would allow him to move freely in the territory occupied by Poole's troops and that this might also somehow be used as a means of getting to meet him personally.

And so it came about. At the next meeting, Lockhart said he was ready to supply Schmidhen with the documents, recommending at the same time that Schmidhen's real surname be given in it. He explained that he would allow him also to use a military pass, when circumstances demanded it, confirming his identity.

There is one further curious detail. Both Lockhart and Cromie were aware that Schmidhen was known in the counter-revolutionary underground movement under a pseudonym and they valued him highly as a fellow conspirator.

Lockhart handed passes for three people to Schmidhen. One of these documents, incidentally, has been preserved and readers of *Nedelya* can see it for themselves.

Thus the required documents found their way into the hands of the Chekists, although no occasion arose to use them. The plans of the conspirators were immediately reported to Dzerjinsky and, as the operation developed, Dzerjinsky conceived the idea of introducing Lockhart to the commanding officer of one of the Lettish regiments who would be of interest to him. E. P. Berzin, Commander of the Lettish Special Section detailed to guard the Kremlin at that time, was selected for this purpose.

Schmidhen introduced Berzin to Lockhart and was present at all their subsequent meetings. The Chekists realized that Lockhart, being a professional agent, had to keep watch on those who were assigned important roles in the execution of the plot. They did their best to prevent discovery of the true purpose of their activities. In particular, Schmidhen only met Berzin by pre-arrangement at agreed places; usually it was at 'Olienii Prudy' or in the grounds of the Sokolniki amusement park.

Lockhart was informed in advance about forthcoming meetings, so that he could organize 'shadowing'. This he did.

The part of E. P. Berzin in discovering the 'Lockhart Plot' is well known. But about Schmidhen nothing is known. Who then is this remarkable Chekist?

He is Jan Janovich Buikis, a Lett and a member of the Party since July, 1917. I am glad to report that Jan Janovich is alive and in good health. He lives in Moscow in a modest flat, the permit for which was handed to him by Dzerjinsky personally. I met him recently. We talked in his small drawing room, one wall of which was decorated with a bronze bas-relief of F. E. Dzerjinsky. When Jan Janovich mentions him, he becomes visibly moved. Generally he is very calm and unflurried yet very agile in spite of his seventy years. He remembers perfectly all the details of those days. Jan Janovich was able to clarify a number of points and to explain many things which have been a mystery until recently.

He was directed into the Cheka in March, 1918 and two months later F. E. Dzerjinsky gave to him the responsible assignment of which we have spoken.

'It was very difficult,' said Jan Janovich. 'The security of the state was in the hands of people with no experience.'

On one occasion he failed to complete on schedule an assignment set him by Dzerjinsky. He was very depressed and, when reporting to the Chairman of the Cheka, asked guiltily to be replaced by a more experienced comrade. Quietly, Dzerjinsky replied that the experience of every Chekist was limited to the few months of the Cheka's existence. He expressed his confidence that the Chekist Buikis would complete the assignment.

Indeed, Dzerjinsky's task was fulfilled. Even today, that clever diplomat and agent, Lockhart, does not know that he had disclosed his anti-Soviet plans to the Chekists.

I asked Jan Janovich how it was that he, a direct participant in this historical operation, still remained unknown. Was it not his own fault? Embarrassed, he answered that he did not consider his participation in unmasking Lockhart as of special merit. This modest reply is characteristic of Jan Janovich Buikis.

Colonel V. Kravchenko

The above version of the role of Buikis, alias Schmidhen, is not convincing. The main point of interest lies in Bruce Lockhart being made out to be the real 'villain' of 1918 while Reilly's role is reduced to the completely minor one of introducing the Letts to Bruce Lockhart. In fact, as Bruce Lockhart makes clear in *Memoirs of a British Agent*, it was he who passed on the Letts to Reilly. Further, my father made it clear in the same book that he was suspicious of Schmidhen all along. In the index to *Memoirs of a British Agent*, he is listed as 'Schmidhen, Soviet Agent'!

Perhaps Schmidhen claimed the credit for foiling the

'Lockhart Plot', but in fact the failure of Reilly's grand coup to overthrow the Bolsheviks was solely due to its betrayal by the Frenchman René Marchand.

The motives behind Soviet propaganda are not always obvious and it could well be that the Russians, in order to forestall any attempt of mine to build up Reilly into a hero in the war against Communism, wished to project him as being a person of no significance.

However, the *Nedelya* article was far from being the end of the matter.

XIII

Of being taken by the insolent foe.

OTHELLO

Three months after publication of the *Nedelya* article, it became abundantly clear that the Russian dossier on Sidney Reilly was still very much in existence. In early June, 1966, there were published in Russia over 2,000,000 copies of a book which claimed to give the whole story of the success of Dzerjinsky and the G.P.U. in capturing Reilly in 1925.

Although undoubtedly published to impress the Russian public – and perhaps the outside world – with the efficiency of the Soviet counter-intelligence services, this later Russian version not only purports to give the truth about Reilly's fate but, unlike the *Nedelya* article, demonstrates quite unequivocally the outstanding importance attached by the Russians to Reilly and to the need to capture Britain's master spy.

A translation of this detailed, although dramatized, account under the title *Troubled Waters* is as follows:

Plots were being hatched in Russia for new intrigues and acts of terrorism. One of the organizers of these anti-Soviet activities was the already well-known

Sidney George Reilly, agent of the British Intelligence Service. It was the G.P.U. under the direction of Dzerjinsky, which foiled Reilly's scheme.

This operation was carried out by 'The Trust'.

Here then are the details of the operation which laid low the plans of Sidney George Reilly, retired officer of the British Air Force, one of the leading agents of the Intelligence Service.

Who was this agent described in the West as 'The Second Lawrence'?

According to information supplied by Reilly himself, he was born in Connemara, Ireland in 1874. According to other sources he was born in Odessa.

Reilly began his business life at Port Arthur in the Far East, as an employee of the timber firm, Gruenberg & Reilly. There, in Port Arthur, he became a director of the Danish West Asiatic Company. Later, after the Russo–Japanese War, he was involved with the firm of Mendrochovich and Schubersky, in supplying armaments to the Russian army. Reilly earned a substantial sum in commission from the German shipbuilding firm of Blohm & Voss, which was engaged in the rebuilding of the Imperial Russian Fleet.

Reilly's command of languages and his knowledge of the German Fleet attracted the attention of the British Intelligence, which had already become interested in him because of his international commercial activities in the field of armaments. In the last years of the First World War, Reilly skilfully deceived the General Staffs of the warring countries and mingled with senior officers of the Germany navy. At the beginning of 1918, the Intelligence Service sent him to Murmansk on an assignment which Reilly considered to be the most important of his life.

It was at this point that the paths of Reilly and Savinkoff crossed. For a long time Savinkoff had been in exile abroad but, following the February Revolution, he had returned to Russia where he was quite uncompromising in his hostility toward the Bolshevik party. It was he who instituted the death penalty for soldiers deserting from the front. He also entered into close contact with the British Intelligence Service, and as a direct consequence, came to meet Sidney George Reilly. The alliance of these two sworn enemies of Soviet power was to continue until Savinkoff's last journey to Russia in 1924.

In the winter of 1917, a certain Monsieur Massino appeared in aristocratic circles. His visiting card proclaimed him to be 'Agent for Turkish and Eastern Countries'. In the spring of the same year, he was to be seen in the cafés and gambling clubs where wine from the Imperial cellars was to be had. His outward appearance was described as follows: 'Monsieur Massino has the face of a man who has lived too well, his eyes are alight with an evil glint and his lips are sensual. He holds himself very straight, despite his years, and is very elegantly dressed.' Only a few knew that the name Massino concealed the identity of Sidney George Reilly, secret agent of the Intelligence Service.

Reilly succeeded in obtaining false documents that gave him entry into a number of Soviet organizations. He had several different addresses, and was quite at home in all stratas of society. Especially was he at home with women.

'If a lieutenant of artillery could manage to blow up the dying embers of the fire of French Revolution, why cannot a lieutenant of the Intelligence Service become dictator of Moscow?' he asked his close friends.

Reilly's plans were ambitious. He took part in the Left Social-Revolutionary insurrection in Moscow of July, 1918. Lockhart has stated that Reilly was with him in his box at the Bolshoi Theatre during a session of the All Russian Congress of the Soviets, when he received the news of the murder of the German Ambassador, Count Mirbach. In fact, Reilly's seat in the box that day was empty, as Reilly was himself taking part in the insurrection staged by the Social-Revolutionaries.

The insurrection was suppressed but, shortly afterwards, Reilly appeared at the head of a new conspiracy to assassinate Lenin and other prominent members of the party.

From November 28th to December 3rd, 1918, the Revolutionary Tribunal sat in Moscow. The accused before the court on this occasion were Robert Bruce Lockhart, head of the English Mission, the French Consul, Grenard, and Lieutenant of the British Intelligence, Sidney George Reilly.

The findings of the Tribunal stated:

'This attempt at a counter-revolution was carried out with cynical disregard for international law and with criminal means to violate extra-territorial privileges. The whole onus rests in the first instance on the capitalist Governments, the responsibility for whose evil purposes lies with the indicted persons. The Revolutionary Tribunal finds R. Lockhart, Grenard and S. G. Reilly to be enemies of the working people and orders them to be shot on their first appearance on Russian Territory.' (Reilly managed to hide before the Tribunal commenced its sittings, while Lockhart and Grenard had already been expelled from Russia.)

On returning to London, Reilly seemed to be out of favour. He was saved through his friendly relations with Winston Churchill and by his colleague in the Moscow conspiracy, George Hill, who had also succeeded in hiding (in Moscow). Under the pretence of being engaged in commerce, Reilly soon returned to the shores of the Black Sea, to the territory occupied by the White Armies and the interventionists.

In 1922, Reilly and Savinkoff organized an attempt to assassinate the Peoples' Commissar George Vassilovich Chicherin and members of the Soviet delegation at The Hague Conference.* The attempt failed only because the Soviet delegation had delayed its departure. Eventually, following their last meeting in Paris, Reilly approved of Savinkoff's clandestine journey to Russia. On August 10th, 1924, he left via Berlin and Warsaw with a Finnish passport in the name of Stepanoff. It was Reilly who subsidized this journey.

On August 29th, the arrest of Savinkoff on Russian territory was announced. He was arrested by Pilar in Minsk and delivered to Moscow. In the courtyard of G.P.U. headquarters, Savinkoff said in muted tones:

'I honour the power and wisdom of the G.P.U.'

Savinkoff's protégés were disillusioned by his

---

* This conference, held in the summer of 1922, was concerned with currency matters. It followed immediately a conference in Genoa which Chicherin attended. He never arrived in The Hague for the second conference.

arrest and his confession of activities against the Soviet Government. His confession in court represented a defeat for Reilly.

In 1924, Reilly set up in business in the U.S.A. under the same of 'Sidney Berns – Indian Linen', and took part in other commercial ventures. While in the U.S.A., he received a letter in code from a Secret Service colleague, announcing the arrival in Paris of a married couple with the name of Krasnostanoff.

'This couple,' the letter stated, 'represent an undertaking which will be of immense importance to the future of European and American markets. The married couple estimate that the business will show results in two years, but certain eventualities make one think even sooner. The business is enormous and widespread and you would be wise to consider it seriously. The couple at the moment refuse to disclose the names of interested parties and take shelter under pretext of security. Apparently these are very important people.' Reilly's correspondent added: 'The matter has the interest of the British and French.'

The name of Krasnostanoff hid the identity of Maria Vladimirovna Zaharchenko Schultz and her husband George Radkevich.

To none of the leaders of the *émigré* organizations did it occur that the emissaries Maria Zaharchenko and her husband had been sent by direction of the G.P.U. in Moscow. Zaharchenko and others who were also sent as emissaries fully believed that they were preparing for a counter-revolution. Even the very experienced Reilly believed in 'The Trust'.

In January, 1925, the G.P.U. gave Yakushev the

assignment of investigating the possibilities of luring Sidney George Reilly to Helsinki and thence to Moscow. 'The Window' across the Finnish frontier, in the region of Sestroretsk, was organized somewhat later. The role of a sympathizer of 'The Trust' movement was played by Toivo Vjahi.

Maria Zaharchenko and her husband, on their return from Paris, were sent to Leningrad. This gave them frequent opportunities to visit Helsinki where they were given a friendly welcome. There were meetings too between the Finnish General Staff and Alexander Alexandrovich Yakushev.

They sat in a restaurant on the esplanade at Helsinki. Through the window they could see, in the winter sunshine, the statue of the poet Iganu Runberg. An observer would have thought them a couple, no longer young, perhaps, but happy and well preserved, outwardly in love, whose romance had endured for years. But if anyone could have heard their conversation he would have realized that no trace of love existed between the two of them.

'Why did the Finns manage to beat the Reds? How did the Finnish barons succeed in cutting off the hydra's head of a Finnish Revolution, while our own Deniken and Wrangel failed? What is your opinion, Alexander Alexandrovich?'

'What do you think?'

'It was because they started hanging too late,' she replied.

'How does one know when it's too late or too early to start?'

'They should have started hanging at the very beginning. Now we do not allow them to do so.

Nevertheless, I do have confidence in Alexander Pavlovich.'

'Of course one must use a heavy hand. I regret, Maria Vladimirovna, that in Paris we did not see the general at the outset. The arrival of Wrangel interfered and made it hopeless. For this reason, we were afterwards unable to reach agreement.'

'Kutyepoff is a strong man. In Gallipoli he hanged a lot – all those who forgot their duty.'

'Nevertheless, how did a General of Cavalry, Baron Mannerheim, manage to do what another General of Cavalry, Skoropadsky, failed to achieve?'

'I was told that the Baron managed to do everything quite perfectly: drink and not get drunk, command a squadron, command a country, but most important – to execute by shooting!'

Yakushev suddenly laughed: 'You are ruthless, Maria Vladimirovna, ruthless, although beautiful . . . For some reason I imagine you in a ball-dress and not in this guise. A teacher and an officer's widow? And you so full of woman's charms! Incidentally, you have a minister's head on your shoulders and for that reason I forgive your complaints. And also because when you speak of a future Emperor you have an expression . . .'

'What sort of expression?'

'Well, radiant! . . . of the future Russia, the Russia which we lost, the Russia you and I knew and I believe we will restore!'

'At the price of blood, much blood,' she said. 'By the way, did you ever meet this man Reilly in Petrograd?'

'No, but I met some other English officers – snobs, who strutted about in dinner-jackets.'

'This man, they say, is not at all like that. This man is unflinchingly brave.'

He suddenly grasped her hand and lowering his eyes, said with feeling:

'Maria, poor Maria, you, with your beauty of a daughter of Caucasus, you don't know what a viper you are nursing in your bosom.'

She turned from him in embarrassment but, with a glance, he drew her attention to the next table. A gentleman with a cigar was obviously listening to them.

'Isn't it time for us to go?'

'Let's go!'

In the street, he said:

'Do you think the Finns trust us? They have not forgotten General Bobiekoff, the Governor-General; they also remember the Grand Duke Nicolas Alexandrovich . . . Everywhere we must plan in secrecy, everywhere we must watch. We must learn, Maria Vladimirovna.'

'Learn what – and where?'

'Well, from this man Reilly.' He looked at his watch: 'Time to go to Bunakoff. He is waiting.'

At one o'clock they were at Bunakoff's. He was a British Intelligence agent.

The conversation began in general terms but Yakushev, as usual, managed to direct it to the business in hand.

'You suggested we should get in touch with the English. How should we go about this?'

'I can tell you that someone is coming from England for preliminary discussions.'

'Can you not be more precise – who is it? The "Iron One"?'

228

'He, himself. Are you disappointed?'

'According to reports, the "Iron One" is heavily engaged in commerce. Why should he resume his old life?'

Bunakoff shrugged his shoulders: 'Do you think he can throw up what has cost him the best years of his life? Then you do not know this man. I can tell you Soviet Russia has never had such a dangerous enemy.'

'May God grant it so,' said Maria Zaharchenko.

Bunakoff produced a letter from Reilly. It was signed with the pseudonym 'The Iron One'.

'Red power is slowly but inevitably dying,' he wrote in the letter. 'The heroic period of the spring of 1921, which was followed by a period of consolidation, did not produce the anticipated results in view of the terrible national famine and economic breakdown. It is the Red army which, up to now, seems to me to be the enigma. The fundamental question is: which is going faster – the infiltration into the army of a healthy-minded peasant element or the entry of Communist recruits? In the first stages of the counter-revolution, probably the most important thing to deal with will be the special sections of the G.P.U. I have little reliable information about them but suggest that on account of their numerical inferiority they could not, at the moment of our success, swim against the stream in face of a mutiny by the army. That is to say, they would be forced to yield to the wishes of the masses.'

Reilly advised a programme of propaganda and terrorism, but one unanswered question remained. At what price could moral and material help be obtained from Europe and America?

'As for myself, I can only say the following,' wrote

Reilly, 'this matter is the most important thing in my life. I am ready to serve in every possible way I can.'

The contents of the 'Iron One's' letter became known to the G.P.U. It was then that the need to capture Reilly was decided upon.

Reilly's plans could have been put into operation by Bunakoff, but Reilly insisted that he should be invited to Helsinki to assist in espionage and intelligence work.

Somehow, Yakushev had to win Bunakoff's confidence. An unexpected incident helped.

'My brother, Boris Biboliavich, lives in Moscow. Would it be possible to send him my greetings?' asked Bunakoff in the course of a meeting with Yakushev.

'Possibly,' said Yakushev pretending to think about something else. 'But why shouldn't you see him yourself?'

'You're not going to order me to go to Moscow straight into the arms of the G.P.U., are you?'

'Why go to Moscow? He could come to you in Helsinki.'

'Is that possible?'

Yakushev laughed.

'That we can arrange, dear fellow. We will deliver your brother whole and unhurt.'

And in August, 1925, a touching meeting took place between the brothers Bunakoff.

Boris Bunakoff informed his elder brother how his journey to Finland had been accomplished. It had been all very simple. One evening he was called for, given half an hour to get ready and taken to the station. The following morning he was in Leningrad. In the evening he reached Sestroretsk and late at night a 'bribed' frontier guard took him across the Finnish frontier. On the Finnish side of the border, Captain Rusensterm and his brother were waiting for him. The most unpleasant part of the journey had been a walk along a very muddy road!

Naturally, all the arrangements for the younger Bunakoff to cross the frontier had been planned in minute details by Chekists. But the elder Bunakoff's confidence in 'The Trust' now increased. He considered himself indebted to Yakushev for making possible the meeting with his brother.

It appears that Reilly wanted to meet members of 'The Trust' as early as May, 1925, but he was prevented from doing so owing to pressure of private business. In the middle of August, 1925, Kutyepoff arrived in Helsinki to renew his contacts with 'The Trust' and to discuss the line he should take with Reilly, who was expected in Paris shortly.

Kutyepoff complained about the intrigues at the court of Nicolai Nikolaievich and said that the army was deserting Wrangel. When he learnt that the Chief of the Polish Deuxieme Bureau,* Talinkorsky, was due in Helsinki to meet Yakushev, he became convinced that 'The Trust' was genuine.

It was decided at the conference that Kutyepoff should receive Reilly in Paris, and from there send him on to Finland. Afterwards Yakushev would invite him to Moscow.

Reilly duly arrived in Paris and met Kutyepoff. They did not take to each other. Reilly was disil-

* The Polish Secret Service.

231

lusioned with the White *émigrés*, and had a poor opinion of their activities. He now pinned his hopes on 'internal forces' – hence his increasing interest in 'The Trust'.

Reilly was expected in Helsinki at the end of September and Maria Zaharchenko sent a message to this effect to Yakushev in Moscow.

On September 21st, 1925, Yakushev was at the Finnish frontier and on September 25th, 1925, Yakushev and Reilly met for the first time at Bunakoff's flat.

Reilly appeared to trust Yakushev and, when Yakushev reminded him of one Milochka Uriev, he relaxed and lapsed into personal reminiscences. In short, it was a friendly and affable meeting.

Yakushev wrote in his report: 'Reilly was dressed in a grey coat and in a faultless grey check suit. He made an unpleasant impression: there was something cruel in the keen look of the black eyes, the hard lower lip. He was very elegant. His attitude in conversation was very reserved. He sat in the armchair, corrected the crease in his trousers, and adjusted his socks in his new yellow shoes. He started by stating that, for the present, it was impossible for him to go to Russia but that he would go in two or three months' time to establish relations with "The Trust".'

I said: 'What a pity to have made the journey all the way from America almost to Wyborg and to stop on the threshold . . .'

Reilly declared his intention of leaving on Saturday on the ship for Stettin. As he only had until September 30th, there was nothing he could achieve in the time. He could not delay his departure.

Yakushev was disappointed, realizing that the plan which had been worked out in such detail had broken down. Reilly had said, 'In two or three months,' but much could happen in that time. There was the constant danger of a failure, for alongside those who were loyal were Staynitzin's emissaries. Then there was the problem of the convinced monarchists such as Mukaloff who had arrived for the second time from Moscow. All this worried Yakushev.

'When Reilly announced,' wrote Yakushev in his report, 'that at the present time he could not make the journey, I said, as quickly as possible, that if it was a question of speed, I was prepared to arrange the trip to Moscow in such a way that he could be in Leningrad on Saturday morning and leave there for Moscow the same evening. A whole day would be ample to get acquainted with the Political Council of "The Trust". Then in the evening he could return to Leningrad, spend Monday there, and that night, pass through "The Window" back to Helsinki. That would be on the Tuesday, and on the Wednesday there was a ship leaving for Stettin.'

After listening to Yakushev, Reilly became thoughtful. Probably he longed to surprise his colleagues in the Intelligence Service and go to Moscow, despite the sentence of death which had been hanging over his head since 1918. He had confidence in 'The Trust', especially after the meeting with Kutyepoff and Maria Zaharchenko, and also because he was aware of the organization's contacts with the Finnish, Estonian and Polish Intelligence Services.

We will return to Yakushev's report: 'After thinking for a while, Reilly said: "All right, you have convinced me. I'll go with you." Bunakoff rose in surprise. I suggested we should discuss arrangements for the journey and said, "Your overcoat and suit will attract attention in Russia – take Radkevich's overcoat. We must also buy a cap and top boots. Leave your things with Bunakoff – you will only need a small suitcase. I can promise you quite a comfortable journey and a completely safe one.""

When all had been decided, Reilly became voluble. He asked questions about 'The Trust', about life in Russia and about the Soviet attitude toward religion. He was full of advice and made out a case for the inevitability of Jewish pogroms after the counterrevolution. He insisted, however, that the new Government should in no way be seen to be connected with such a programme. The future form of the Government, he said, would have to be monarchist with a dictatorship to restore order. The Grand Duke Nicolai Nikolaievich would become the symbol of power.

Yakushev was pretending to be a senior member of the counter-revolutionary organization and said that 'The Trust' was relying on Reilly's assistance to obtain funds, which were needed to continue the fomenting of unrest and the bribing of officials.

Reilly replied that he had plans ready and would give full details of these to the Political Council in Moscow.

Before changing into more modest clothes, Reilly admired himself in front of the mirror:

'What a magnificent suit, isn't it?'

Via Bunakoff, he sent a letter to his wife: 'I am leaving tonight and will return on Tuesday morning.

234

There is no risk at all. If by chance I should be arrested in Russia it will be merely an unimportant coincidence. My new friends are so powerful that they will succeed in freeing me.'

Reilly took leave of the Bunakoff's, Maria Zaharchenko and Radkevich who remained in Finland.

Reilly was conducted to the frontier by Rusensterm and Radkevich. At ten p.m. on September 25th, they arrived at Kuokalla Station. On the stroke of midnight they made their way to the frontier. Reilly's top-boots squeaked. To stop this, he wetted the soles of his boots in a ditch.

When they arrived at the River Sestri, a shadow appeared on the river bank. This was Toivo Vjahi – one of the most experienced agents of the Soviet frontier service – who was pretending to be a frontier guard who had been bribed. He had precise instructions to take Reilly by cart from the frontier to Pargolovo Station, seventeen kilometres away, and on from there by train. If Reilly had changed his mind and started to resist, Toivo Vjahi would have used his gun. While crossing the river, Reilly paused and started to talk in English to his guides from Finland. He soon stopped when Vjahi told him that it was no place for such discussions.

Then began a tiring walk to the cart waiting for them in the forest. The road was terrible and the cart jolted Reilly so severely that he could stand it no longer. He jumped out and trudged through the squelching mud for the whole seventeen kilometres to Pargolovo Station where Vjahi put him on the train for Leningrad. There he was received by Schukin (an agent of the G.P.U.) and Yakushev.

Schukin gave Reilly a passport in the name of Steinberg.

On the way to Leningrad, Reilly spoke to Yakushev about Savinkoff. The rumours in *émigré* circles that Savinkoff had been killed seemed illogical. A man such as Savinkoff could not exist without plotting 'affairs' of some kind. Reilly considered him to be a conspirator *par excellence*, but said he could never get on with other people. In Reilly's opinion, Savinkoff was too slow to overcome difficulties. He liked comfort, women, and was an inveterate gambler. He was quite unscrupulous in his methods of obtaining means for a 'cushy' life. In the end, Savinkoff had been very much on his own: his assistants were neither wise nor loyal and he had no real staff. These were the main reasons for his ruin.

'If,' said Reilly, 'he had such an organization as "The Trust" he would be unbeatable. The man had charm, he had won over Churchill, Pilsudsky and the French.'

On the morning of September 26th, Sidney Reilly was in Leningrad where he spent the day in Schukin's flat. He was introduced to a factory hand, a deputy of the Moscow Soviet – Staroff – who gave accounts of 'working conditions'. Also present was Mukaloff, one of Wrangel's representatives.

That evening, Reilly, Yakushev and Mukaloff left by International Sleeping Car for Moscow. Staroff had preceded them.

On the platform in Moscow, the guest was awaited by Dorojinsky, Schadkorsky and Staroff – 'delegate of the monarchist organization' – but in reality from the G.P.U.

September 27th was a Sunday. In a *datcha* at

Malahovka a conference took place with the Political Council of 'The Trust'. Even the Chief of Staff, Nicolai Nicolaievich Potapoff was present.

Lieutenant-General Potapoff, late of the General Staff, made a big impression on Reilly. Also present was Alexander Langovoi – Commander of the Red army. After lunch, the party went into the woods and settled down on the grass in the shade of the trees. Yakushev raised the question of financial help.

Reilly said: 'No Government will give you money. Today, everyone's house is on fire. Churchill believes, as I do, in the speedy overthrow of Soviet power, but he is not in a position to supply funds. He has been keenly disappointed on a number of occasions. For us, the most important thing is to put out the fire in our own house. In the colonies there is unrest. The workers are moving to the left due to the influence of Moscow. Money must, therefore be sought inside Russia. My plans to raise money are crude and will probably repel you.'

Then Sidney Reilly announced his plan.

'In Russia there are great treasures of immense value. I am thinking of old master paintings, engravings, precious stones, gems. To remove these from the museums will not be too difficult. Just think of the money – which would amount to many thousands of pounds! Abroad, such treasures have a tremendous value. It is true that it is difficult to steal from the public rooms of the museums, but in the basements, ready and packed, are some amazing works of art. We must arrange to send these abroad. I myself, without the help of any intermediaries, can organize their sale. In this way, we can obtain very substantial sums.'

Potapoff exclaimed: 'But this would ruin the reputation of our whole organization. We are not museum robbers!'

This remark made no impression on Reilly whatsoever.

'For the sake of money, a reputation may have to be sacrificed. In any case, it will not be necessary to let more than a few into the secret.'

He then brought out a written note listing what had to be stolen:

1. Pictures of famous Dutch painters, also French masters and important Rembrandts.

2. Engravings of French and English masters of the XVIIIth century, and miniatures of the XVIIIth and XIXth centuries.

3. Antique coins of gold, silver and bronze.

4. Italian and Flemish primitives.

5. Works of the great masters of the Italian and Spanish Schools.

Potapoff and Yakushev had difficulty in keeping quiet when they heard these proposals.

Reilly continued: 'Another method of raising money is by working for English Intelligence. First and foremost, I am interested in obtaining intelligence about the Comintern. 'The Trust' must infiltrate into the Comintern. Is this difficult? With determination it should be possible. If information about the Comintern cannot be obtained then it must be forged. The letter from the Chairman of the Comintern gave the Conservatives the possibility of victory at the General Election. Some may insist that it was a forgery but results were more important!'

Reilly's spirits rose. He was in Moscow. He was being treated like a V.I.P. and being listened to by the Chiefs of 'The Trust' as if he were an oracle. He already had a big reputation with the Intelligence Service, but that was not everything. He could make a career such as Mussolini had made for himself. Was he any better than Sidney George Reilly?

In the forest, it was getting damp. The sun was setting.

They returned to the *datcha*.

On the way, Reilly drew Yakushev aside: 'You have the good manners of a gentleman who looks at things more realistically than the rest of the members of "The Trust".'

Under a pledge of strict secrecy Reilly informed Yakushev that he had a source from whom he could obtain fifty thousand dollars. Reilly said he would provide this money on condition that it was used to organize the theft of pictures and other valuables from museums and also for infiltrating into the Comintern.

'General Potapoff is clearly too scrupulous. I must tell you that in an affair of this kind – I am speaking of a counter-revolution – you will never succeed if you observe the rules of morality. Take terrorism, for instance. Savinkoff once told me that one of his terrorists failed to throw a bomb into a carriage because there were children in it. If you are going to be influenced by principles in your fight with the Soviets, you will achieve nothing. But let's not talk only of terrorism. I look upon my activities from a much wider standpoint – not only from the viewpoint of politics, but also as a businessman. I want to interest you in this deal. You won't overthrow Soviet power in three months. We must prepare a thorough plan for the 'export' of art treasures. I have personal

239

influence with the press. When I return from Moscow, I will offer *The Times* a series of articles under the title of *The Great Bluff*. Of course this will mean another visit to Russia – and not only one. We must collect documents, facts, figures or else we shall not be believed.'

He looked at his watch. He had to leave for Leningrad by the evening train, cross the frontier during the night and proceed thence to Helsinki in order to catch the Wednesday boat to Stettin. Reilly took leave of Yakushev, Potapoff and others. Two motorcars were waiting. Reilly took a seat in the first car together with Puzitsky (an experienced Chekist who took part in the arrest of Savinkoff) and Staroff.

Potapoff and Yakushev were in the second car. They gave vent to their feelings.

'What a terrible man!' said Potapoff.

Yakushev told him of his conversation with Reilly when they had been alone. Both men were shaken. (Neither incidentally, was ever to see Sidney George Reilly again.) . . .

It had been planned to arrest Reilly in the car while on the way to Moscow but he wanted to send a postcard to his friends abroad and to put it with his own hand into the pillar-box to prove that he had visited Moscow. In order to find out to whom the card was to be addressed, Reilly was taken to the flat of one of the G.P.U. agents taking part in the operation.

While Reilly was writing his postcard, Staroff telephoned G.P.U. headquarters to report the delay. He received orders to arrest Reilly as soon as he had mailed his postcard.

Reilly was then arrested and taken to G.P.U. headquarters. At the preliminary interrogation, conducted by Pilar, Reilly admitted his identity and that he had entered Soviet territory illegally with the aid of 'The Trust', a counter-revolutionary monarchist organization. He refused to explain his criminal behaviour.

When, in the course of the interrogation, Reilly learnt that 'The Trust' was an operation of Soviet Intelligence, he lost his self-control and could not conceal his distress.

Reilly was locked up in solitary confinement in the 'Inner Prison'. There he remained for just over a month.

On the Moroseika, in Staunitz's flat, Yakushev learned of Reilly's arrest. His first thought was for the future of 'The Trust'. Undoubtedly Reilly's arrest would lead the counter-revolutionaries to lose confidence in Yakushev. Yet 'The Trust' was still needed: Kutyepoff had faith in it and even Wrangel did.

On the night of September 28th/29th, therefore, Puzitsky and some colleagues left for Leningrad. On the frontier, near Allekul, a shooting incident was faked. There was firing and considerable noise as a scene was staged purporting to show that Reilly and his companions had been ambushed and that Reilly had been killed in the ensuing mêlée.

In accordance with a prearranged plan, the genuine members of 'The Trust' were not to be told anything immediately of the incident on the frontier. It was intended that the first news about the catastrophe should come from Finland. Only then would the alarm be sounded among 'The Trust' generally.

On September 29th, a telegram was received from

Maria Zaharchenko saying: 'The parcel has disappeared. We await explanation.'

Reilly was in solitary confinement. He hoped that the Intelligence Service of the British Government would insist on his release by the Soviet Union. At the same time one thought agitated him: after the failure of 1918 and after Savinkoff's desertion, would he manage to get out of the mess?

He wanted to believe that they would take into consideration his services in the First World War when he had penetrated into the German Army disguised as a General Staff officer and had obtained valuable information for British Intelligence.

Again and again he considered his position. 'The Trust' had proved itself amazingly adept at deception: Grand Duke Nicolai Nicolaievich had faith in it as did Kutyepoff and Wrangel. Most important of all, the Intelligence Services of the Baltic countries, of France and even of England had confidence in it. Reilly had always considered the British Intelligence Service to be the finest in the world. No-one could deny its many years of glory and then suddenly – the Cheka. It was amazing that an organization which had been in existence for only seven years could have carried through such a complicated operation. As an experienced intelligence agent himself, Reilly had to acknowledge the accomplished skills of Yakushev and Staroff. If he had been unable to see through them, how then could Maria Zaharchenko and her husband be expected to do so? That the latter had joined 'The Trust' in the dark as to its real purposes, he was convinced. He had complete confidence in Zaharchenko. He well knew her relationship with Kutyepoff.

Sidney George Reilly, himself on the verge of fifty, was astonished that such comparatively young men had undertaken the operation. Artuzoff was only thirty-three at the time, Pilar, thirty-one and Staroff, twenty-eight. They had only been working as intelligence agents for a short time – not more than six or seven years. Reilly was amazed at the aptitude, skill and 'artistry' of Staroff. In acting the role of a factory worker and deputy of the Moscow Soviet, he had played the part of an upstart brilliantly.

Many hours were spent in talks with Reilly. The accused realized that as all was now known he could only confirm the charges levelled against him.

Yet Reilly continued to believe that he would be released. He wanted to return to England as a hero, having safeguarded all the secrets of British Intelligence.

FROM THE PROTOCOL OF THE
INTERROGATION OF
S. G. REILLY – OCTOBER 7th, 1925

On October 7th, 1925, I interrogated in the capacity of Prosecutor, Reilly, Sidney George, born 1874, British subject, born Connemara (Ireland); father, captain in the navy. Permanent residence, London and, more recently, New York. Captain in the British army. Wife abroad. Education: university; studied at Heidelberg in the faculty of philosophy; in London, the Royal Institute of Mines, specializing in chemistry. Party: active Conservative. Was judged *in absentia* in the matter of Lockhart in 1918.

Later in the protocol, the story is told of Reilly's activities after he had managed to escape in 1918.

Afterwards, I was appointed political officer for South Russia and went to Denikin's Headquarters; I was in the Crimea, in the South-East and at Odessa. I remained in Odessa until the end of March 1919. By order of the British High Commissioner in Constantinople, I was instructed to report on Denikin's front and on South Russia generally. Afterwards, I was sent to the Peace Conference in Paris.

From 1919 to 1920 I had close links with various *émigré* groups. At the same time, for the British Government, I undertook negotiations with Jazoschinsky* and Bark† for very important financial plans for backing commercial undertakings and industrial schemes etc. All this time I was in the employ of the Secret Service, my main duties being to advise the ruling circles of England on Russian questions and problems.

At the end of 1920 I was in close contact with Savinkoff and went to Warsaw, where he was organizing an expedition into White Russia. I took part in this expedition and was in Soviet Russian Territory. I received orders to return to London.

In 1923 and 1924, I had to give a lot of my time to my own affairs. In the fight against the Soviet Powers I was less active, although I wrote a good

---

* Jazoschinsky had been a Russian banker before the Revolution and subsequently acted as financial adviser to the White Russians.
† Peter Bark, G.C.V.O., had been the Tsar's Minister of Finance and became, after the war, chief adviser on Central European matters to Montagu Norman, the Governor of the Bank of England. He was a co-director of Bruce Lockhart in the Anglo–Austrian Bank.

deal for the papers (English) and supported Savin-koff. I continued to advise ruling circles in England on Russian questions and in America also, as in those years I was often in the United States. I spent 1925 in New York.

At the end of 1925, I illegally crossed the Finnish frontier, proceeded to Leningrad and after that came to Moscow, where I was arrested.

FROM THE PROTOCOL OF INTERROGATION OF S. G. REILLY ON OCTOBER 9th, 1925

I arrived in Soviet Russia on my own initiative, hearing from Bunakoff of the existence of an apparently important anti-Soviet group.

I have always been actively engaged in anti-Bolshevik matters and to these I have given much time and my personal funds. I can state that the years 1920–4, for instance, cost me at a very minimum calculation fifteen thousand to twenty thousand pounds.

I was well-informed about Russian affairs from information sent to me by various sources in Russia and by English and American intelligence sources.

In this deposition, it should be noted that Reilly arrived in Russia 'on his own initiative'. Later he was to reveal his ties with London. The initiative of 'The Trust' was only a stimulant to the trip.

Prior to his arrest, Reilly once said to Yakushev that he knew all the English secret agents working in Soviet offices but during his cross-examinations he stubbornly denied this. He talked much of general subjects, forgetting that he was the accused and not a consultant on Russian affairs. Those he used to advise were no longer interested in his fate. But when Reilly was told of the decision of the G.P.U. to carry out the supreme penalty, i.e. to carry out the death sentence passed on him in 1918, his former courage failed him.

On October 13th he wrote the following statement:

TO THE PRESIDENT OF THE G.P.U.
F. E. DZERJINSKY

After prolonged deliberation, I express willingness to give you complete and open acknowledgement and information on matters of interest to the G.P.U. concerning the organization and personnel of the British Intelligence Service and, so far as I know it, similar information on American Intelligence and likewise about Russian *émigrés* with whom I have had business.

Moscow. The Inner Prison   Sidney Reilly
30th October, 1925

He no longer had any hope of intervention by the English Government. He only wanted to live – at any price, even at the price of disclosing all the secrets of his employers. His 'high ideals', 'philosophical ideas' – the planning of provocation, diversions and terrorism – all these were thrown aside. To save his life – for the sake of this, Reilly was ready to sacrifice everything.

One can imagine what this man must have gone through in the sleepless nights. It was not so long ago that in a Paris night-club he and Savinkoff had drunk to the latter's safe return from Russia, had ogled the girls lifting their legs in a frenzied can-can in the hurly-burly of Montmartre at night . . . Savinkoff was no more . . .

Reilly complained of sleeplessness and a doctor was called to him. Once when talking to Pilar, Reilly said that if the counter-revolution had succeeded in 1918 – or later, the Reds would hardly have been treated as humanely as he, Reilly, was being treated.

The sentence of execution of the Revolutionary Tribunal was carried out on November 5th, 1925.

After the arrest of Reilly 'The Trust' passed through a difficult period.

Maria Zaharchenko was trying to reach Moscow, hoping that Reilly was only wounded, and was in hospital, and hoping at any price to save him.

She wrote Yakushev: 'There is a torturing, dark, loneliness, full of the unknown . . . I cannot get rid of the feeling that I somehow betrayed Reilly and was responsible for his death myself. I was responsible for "The Window". For the sake of the movement, I ask to be allowed to work inside Russia.'

She was promised that she would be called to Moscow.

Reilly's wife, Pepita Bobadilla, arrived in Helsinki. She met Maria Zaharchenko, showed her the last letter from Reilly which she had received via Bunakoff and in which he himself admitted the possibility of arrest. Maria Zaharchenko convinced Pepita that 'The Trust' had not been responsible in any way for Reilly's fate.

Pepita believed this. She inserted an obituary

notice in the *Daily Express** announcing the death of Sidney George Reilly, on the Finnish Frontier, at the village of Allekul, on the night of 28th/29th September, 1925.

In the flat of Staunitz,† immediately after the arrest, the alarm was sounded. Yakushev, Langovoi, Suboff, Staunitz and Mukaloff gathered together. The scene was staged for Mukaloff and Staunitz, who did not know what had actually happened to Reilly. Mukaloff was absolutely broken, people smoked nervously, various papers were being burnt, cigarette ends lay on the floor. Yakushev wanted to get to Leningrad but he was kept back: he above all others was needed by 'The Trust'. Suboff and Mukaloff set off instead. They were instructed to find out what had happened on the night of September 19th at the frontier. Mukaloff was shown the telegram from Maria Zaharchenko and the following reply was drafted: 'The illness ended with the death of the children.'

From Finland, Maria Zaharchenko was awaited, but Radkevich arrived instead.

He demanded an explanation from Staunitz.

'What happened to Reilly?'

His eyes shone; he held his hand in his pocket, as if he was holding a gun.

Staunitz was overcome and asked Radkevich to give such details of Reilly's fate as were known on the Finnish side of the frontier.

Radkevich pulled himself together and told how,

---

* It was, in fact, *The Times* (see p. 193).
† The pseudonym which Edward Opperput adopted while working as a member of the G.P.U. team involved in 'The Trust' operation.

at the appointed hour, he and Captain Rusensterm walked up to the frontier, waited there and suddenly heard screams and shots. They rushed to the river, thinking that a wounded man was coming across. Never imagining that this could have happened to Reilly and his companions they decided the shots must have been at bandits. In vain they waited by the River Sestrie until morning. From the Russian side of the frontier only mounted frontier guards could be seen.

Radkevich completely accepted this account of the catastrophe at the village of Allekul as the right one and was allowed to re-cross the frontier through 'The Window' in the region of Stolpzoff.

Whereas in many respects this account of Reilly's capture, confessions and eventual execution has the ring of truth, there are many inconsistencies with earlier accounts and, if the whole truth were known inside Russia, many glaring and unnecessary inaccuracies.

The obvious Russian propaganda over Soviet skill in capturing Reilly at all and the decrying of Reilly's character are to be expected. The but passing references to Staunitz (Opperput) who played a major part in the operation are also understandable in view of his later defection.

The account is both strangely accurate and inaccurate about Reilly's personal history. If he 'confessed' to the G.P.U., as the Russians assert, then he certainly told a semi-fictional tale. It was Margaret who had claimed to have a captain in the Navy as a father. Reilly had studied neither in Heidelberg nor in London. He was never in Moscow in the winter of 1927. He never used the name Sidney Berns in the U.S.A.

There may be some truth in the claim that Reilly planned to raise funds by looting Russian museums. Certainly, General Spears, who knew little of Reilly's secret activities, recalls that Reilly had a plan to bring out of Russia valuable old coins and other antiques. To Lieutenant-Colonel Thwaites, who by 1925 was no longer in the S.I.S., Reilly had spoken of recovering Napoleonic treasures cached in Moscow.

His execution is stated to have taken place on November 5th, 1925. And yet the only other date ever previously given by Russia for his death was in *Izvestia*, in September, 1927, when the Russian newspaper stated he had been executed in June of that year with a group of Russian nobles. Except for the original Russian version that Reilly was killed on the Finnish frontier in September 1925, all other Russian references to him have indicated that he was certainly alive in 1926 while one account implied that he was free and at large in 1927. Taking all the other evidence into consideration the statement that he was executed in November 1925 is not convincing.

There is, of course, a further possibility. When Savinkoff returned to Russia in 1924, Reilly suggested in his first letter to the *Morning Post* that Savinkoff had not been captured at all, that he had been killed at the Russian frontier and that the G.P.U. had staged a mock trial with one of their own agents as the chief actor. Did the G.P.U. take note of Reilly's theory and apply it in his own case?

Although it is inconceivable that the above account could have been published in Russia without official approval or instigation, it is still not an 'official statement' of the Soviet Government. The author's several requests recently made to Soviet officials for a simple statement as to the date and place of Reilly's death have, like every similar request for the past forty years, been met with stony silence.

It seems that we are no nearer to knowing the truth about Sidney Reilly's fate than at the time of his disappearance in 1925. The suggestion that he might have defected to the Communists is unthinkable to anyone who knew him at all well and is absurd when applied to a man who devoted so much of his life and most of his wealth to combating Communism. He could scarcely be alive today: he would be ninety-three.

Perhaps the Russians either do not know the whole truth themselves or, having something they consider so important to hide, still wish, even today, to maintain a smoke-screen over Reilly's ultimate fate by issuing deliberately false information. The answer may lie buried in the Communist secret archives in Loubianka Square. If so, it is time the Soviet Government issued an official account of what befell a worthy foe. It would be fascinating to know why in forty years it has felt itself unable to do so.

Whether or not the Russians would give the whole truth in any official statement is another question. Perhaps the publication of this book will itself prompt them into saying something further. In the absence of any official statement, we must continue to wonder what it is the Soviet Government wishes to hide. Can it be that Reilly did escape? Perhaps there is an element in the life of Reilly which remains a closed book to this day – even to the Russians.

The fate of Sigmund Rosenblum, the bastard of

Odessa, who emerged from the jungles of Brazil to become Britain's master spy, is probably destined to be for ever shrouded in mist. The man whose life was so full of mystery would probably himself have wished it to end where it began – in mystery.